MW01492634

The Impossible Dream

The Founding of The Milton S. Hershey Medical Center
of
The Pennsylvania State University

C. Max Lang

George T. Harrell Professor Emeritus and founding chair
Department of Comparative Medicine
College of Medicine
The Milton S. Hershey Medical Center
of
The Pennsylvania State University
Hershey, Pennsylvania

authorHOUSE®

AuthorHouse™
1663 Liberty Drive
Bloomington, IN 47403
www.authorhouse.com
Phone: 1-800-839-8640

First published by AuthorHouse 1/6/2010

ISBN: 978-1-4490-5019-1 (e)
ISBN: 978-1-4490-5017-7 (sc)
ISBN: 978-1-4490-5018-4 (hc)

Library of Congress Control Number: 2009913956

Printed in the United States of America
Bloomington, Indiana

This book is printed on acid-free paper.

Dedicated to my loving wife, Sylvia, and our children Karen, John and Susan

Acknowledgements:

Ms. Anne Robbins Aregood
For transcribing the oral interviews

Ms. Susan Alger, Dr. Joseph Brechbill,&
Mr. James McMahon, Department of
School History, Milton Hershey School

Ms. Michelle Hoffer & Ms. Lisa Piergallini, Hershey
Trust Company

Dr. Graham Jeffries, University Professor and founding
chair, Department of Medicine

Dr. Elliott Vesell, Evan Pugh Professor and Bernard
B. Brodie Professor and founding chair,
Department of Pharmacology
For their critical review of several drafts of the manuscript,
historical data, and insights.

Table of Contents

Preface

The "Impossible Dream" describes the people and events leading to establishment of a new medical school and its teaching hospital in South Central Pennsylvania; the College of Medicine, The Milton S. Hershey Medical Center of The Pennsylvania State University in Hershey, PA. This medical center probably would not have been built if not for a unique set of circumstances. As years passed, the people involved in this project began to forget certain details of the early planning and construction. I decided to preserve these facts and details by recording oral interviews with some of the key participants. All of those invited graciously agreed to reconsider our early history and their role in it. They agreed that these interviews would remain confidential until they approved release of this information. Those wishes have now been met. The author has personally interviewed most of the individuals directly involved in the establishment of the medical center, reviewed all available documents and files, and gathered many recollections. Obviously, a number of other people involved could not be included in this narrative because of a lack of opportunity to interview them and/or review their files. I carefully limited the information contained herein to that which could be substantiated or clearly indicated as a supposition.

Chapter I – People

Milton S. Hershey

Born: September 13, 1857
Died: October 13, 1945
Education: Fourth grade
Position: Hershey Chocolate Co.
President

circa 1932

Much has been written about Mr. Hershey, based often on anecdotal information, some of it embellished. Apparently, he revealed little about his personal feelings. This much is known: his love and devotion to his wife Kitty (Catherine Elizabeth Sweeney); his candy business; his employees and the community in which they worked and lived; and his "boys school", which, in many ways, reflected his own boyhood, i.e. poor, white, male orphans between ages 4-8, later 4-14. Mr. Hershey was not an orphan, *per se*, but his father (Henry) was frequently absent from home, seeking his fortune. He was raised primarily by his mother (Fanny), a stern, conservative, Mennonite lady.

Mr. Hershey spoke very little about his early childhood, and wrote even less. This may have encouraged others to speculate, or even embellish on what really happened--or didn't happen. Some of these stories probably were told during Mr. Hershey's lifetime but there is no evidence that he made any effort to dissuade such stories if he heard

1

them. This may have been a trait picked up by the other Hershey people. I once asked Mr. Arthur Whiteman, who was very close to Mr. Hershey, why they did not openly squelch many of the rumors that floated around the town from time to time. His reply was "...there will always be rumors, including some that are so outrageous you wonder how anyone could believe them. 'We' always believed that it would be a waste of our time to dispel these rumors because they would only start new ones."

The following stories about Mr. Hershey were told to me by Mr. Arthur Whiteman:

> He often felt the sting of being underprivileged. On the rare occasions that he ate out with his mother, they were usually seated behind a post or pillar because they were not dressed as well as the other diners. This treatment engrained a feeling of compassion in him for poor people in unfortunate circumstances, so much so, that he instructed the architect of Hotel Hershey that NO posts or pillars should appear in the main dining room. Later in life he was always well-dressed. One person recalled that if you put a tuxedo on him, he could pass with the best of them.
>
> Mr. Hershey was generous to his employees, perhaps to a fault (his estate was less than $50,000 when he died). He expected his employees to earn their pay, have high moral standards and demonstrate ethical conduct. Anything less, usually led to immediate dismissal. One day, a payday, the bank was unusually busy and when a thunderstorm developed, someone turned on the gas lights so that they could see better to count the money. Mr. Hershey came into the bank after the brief storm and the sun had come out, but the lights were still on. He demanded to know who was responsible for the lights being on. After the situation had been explained to him, he relented and did not fire anyone. Another time, he noticed that the custodian in the bank had

done a poor job of mopping the floor and there was a noticeable build-up of debris and soap scum in the junction between the floor and walls and in corners. The custodian was promptly fired. Mr. Hershey did not tolerate lazy people but was willing always to listen to reason. He did not hesitate to discharge anyone who was dishonest, deceitful, immoral, or disloyal. He demanded honesty, loyalty, and a good day's work.

Mr. Hershey was quite frugal. He and his wife frequently entertained out of town guests by taking them to one of his attractions, such as the Hershey Theatre. Upon arriving, he would go to the front of the line and pay for the tickets for him and his wife. This left the guests (who thought that they were going to be treated) with no choice but to buy their own tickets. Mr. Hershey, of course, recouped his money, and theirs, because he owned the business. Another example of his frugality was that he set a limit of $1,000 per year on the fee that the Hershey Trust Company could charge for administering the assets of the Milton Hershey School – a figure that persists to this day.

Mr. Hershey was known to take risks. For example, he had to borrow money to complete construction of the chocolate factory, a considerable risk since he did not know if it would be successful but he did have confidence in himself. On one occasion the sugar markets collapsed (Mr. Hershey had bought a large stock of sugar at 20 cents a pound and, after the collapse of the market, it was selling for 3 cents a pound) As a result, he had to take out a large loan from a New York bank to meet his financial obligations. Because of the size of the loan the New York bank sent a representative to oversee operation of the chocolate business. It infuriated Mr. Hershey to have someone looking over his shoulder. He instructed his people to pay off the loan as soon as possible. He was willing to take risks but he also bore responsibility.

Mr. Hershey acquired the traits of both his parents: vision and imagination from his father, and thrift and steadfastness from his mother. He loved people and gave all of his money away so that his employees could have a better life and to take care of "good little boys." When asked why he was giving all of his money away, he would reply "I'm executing my own will."

Arthur R. Whiteman

circa 1964

Born: July 6, 1909
Died: June 30, 1988
Education: Business College American
    Institute of Banking
Positions: Hershey Trust Company
    Chairman of the
    Board President Hershey
    National Bank
    Chairman of the Board
    President
    Milton Hershey School
    Board of Managers
    M. S. Hershey Foundation
    Board of Managers
    Hershey Estates &
    Subsidiaries
    Chairman of the Board
    Hershey Foods Corporation
    Director

Mr. Whiteman had a major role, perhaps the key role, in making The Milton S. Hershey Medical Center a reality. Mr. Whiteman was born in NC, his mother's home state; and his father was from PA. His father had gone to AL to work in the coal mines when his mother, who was living in NC with her children at the time, received word that her husband was missing, and presumed dead, in a mine accident.. She then decided to return to PA to be close to her husband's family. She worked in a shirt factory in Harrisburg, PA to support her family. The oldest, a daughter age 10, was supposed to be babysitting but when the mother returned home from work one day she found Arthur, age 4, and his sister, age 6, playing in the Susquehanna River. She knew, then, that something had to be done. One day shortly thereafter she took young Arthur on a trolley ride to Hershey, which he enjoyed immensely until he learned that it would be a one-way trip. He adjusted well to the school. He did not see his mother for 3-4 years and infrequently after that. The philosophy at that time was that if the boys went home for a visit they would be treated like royalty and it would be like that "… if they remained at home and did not return to the school." Mr. Whiteman's enrollment number was 38 but there were only 30 boys in the school; the others had left for different reasons.

Mr. Hershey believed that every boy should learn a trade so that he would have something to fall back on in hard times. Mr. Whiteman was on the paint crew, painting houses and barns under adult supervision. He assumed that would be his vocation in life. One summer, when he was painting buildings, word came down that Mr. Hershey had decided to send the boys to the local high school because he did not have enough boys to offer a rounded, high quality high school education. Furthermore, they would have to repeat a grade to make sure they were competitive with the other students already enrolled. Arthur was very unhappy with this decision because he was number two in his class. He did a lot of grumbling. Apparently this unhappiness got back to Mr. Hershey. One day the school superintendent stopped by where the boys were painting and asked for Arthur. He was petrified when he learned that Mr. Hershey had heard of his unhappiness. But the superintendent asked him if he would like to work in the bank. True to Mr. Whiteman's humble nature, he replied that he would do whatever Mr. Hershey thought was best for him. He then embarked on a work-study arrangement, going to school and working in the bank. He was very successful in banking, so much so that he came to the attention of some large banks in New York City. Mr. Hershey told him of some of these inquiries and asked if he would like to work for them. His reply was always "… no, I would rather work for you, Mr. Hershey." I once asked Mr. Whiteman if he considered Mr. Hershey a father figure. His immediate reply was "Oh no, he was a god!" The boys rarely mingled with Mr. Hershey; their contacts were mainly limited to seeing his car coming down the road and running to the fence to catch a glimpse of him and to wave; and an annual breakfast at Mr. Hershey's house, and as guests, at Hershey Park for the remainder of the day. I also asked him if the boy being held by Mr. Hershey in the statue in Founder's Hall was one boy in particular. The statue was commissioned by the alumni and, no the "boy" was a composite because Mr. Hershey would never select a favorite. He added that the statue reflected how Mr. Hershey felt in his heart However, he was once overheard to say that he would give everything he owned to be able to call one of the boys his own.

Mr. Whiteman was appointed to the Milton Hershey School Board of Managers in 1939 at the age of 25. He was the youngest person on the Board. Mr. Whiteman was of large stature and had to have his suits made by a tailor. His clothes and those for Mrs. Whiteman put a strain on their budget because others in their social group were older and made much higher salaries than he. Mrs. Whiteman was very sensitive to this and, in later years, made sure not to "outshine" the younger women because she could sympathize with their circumstances.

Mr. Whiteman was a tireless worker; he worked every evening after dinner for 2-3 hours, most of the day on Saturdays, and 2-3 hours Sunday afternoons. Mrs. Whiteman told me that when they were first married, Mr. Whiteman told her that he had so much to do, and if he could work those extra hours he could do so much more. She agreed. He often joked that it took three men to replace him when he retired.

Mr. Whiteman served on the Board of Managers for 35 years and 1 month , retiring early because he could not bear the thought of serving longer than his benefactor, Mr. Hershey (who served 35 years and 11 months).

Samuel F. Hinkle

Born: July 9, 1900
Died: April 19, 1984
Education: B. S. (Chemistry) – 1922
The Pennsylvania State Univ.
Positions: Hershey Chocolate
Company
President
Board of Directors
Hershey National Bank
Board of Directors
Milton Hershey School
Board of Managers
M.S. Hershey Foundation
Board of Managers
Hershey Estates
Board of Directors

circa 1963

Mr. Hinkle was recruited by Mr. Hershey because of his training in chemistry. He and Mr. Hershey frequently worked together on Mr. Hershey's first love – chocolate (Mr. Hinkle described Mr. Hershey as an "indefatigable researcher" until the end of his life).

Mr. Hershey was very reserved and shared very few of his innermost thoughts with anyone, including Mr. Hinkle. Mr. Hinkle was made Plant Manager and, later, President of the Chocolate Company. Mr. Hinkle, the last person to see Mr. Hershey alive, had just returned from a business trip to Europe and was summoned to Mr. Hershey's bedside for a progress report. Mr. Hershey died the next day.

Mr. Hinkle was appointed to the Milton Hershey School Board of Managers in January, 1948. He had heard rumors about a surplus of funds in the Trust account but was totally surprised by the amount of the surplus when he was appointed to the Board of Managers. He and Mr. Whiteman had long been friends socially as well as business associates. When Mr. Hinkle was appointed to the Board, Mr.

Whiteman immediately shared his concern about the surplus funds with him, suggesting what could be done, including the construction of a medical school. i.e. a major hospital. He persuaded Mr. Hinkle to write a memo to the Chairman of the Board, Mr. John A. Sollenberger, about their thoughts and request that it be put on their next meeting agenda. The memo was never acknowledged and their thoughts did not become an agenda item until Mr. Sollenberger's retirement. Apparently, Mr. Sollenberger did not agree with their assessment that something needed to be done with the surplus funds, how to spend it, or perhaps he had something else in mind.

There is a strong suggestion that Mr. Whiteman was the person behind Mr. Hershey's financial success and the concept of a medical center. However, Mr. Whiteman was a humble, quiet person, and not particularly comfortable speaking before large groups; but was the "power behind the throne." Mr. Hinkle, then became the "point man." Mr. Hinkle was also humble but a forceful person in the business world. The combination of Mr. Whiteman and Mr. Hinkle became formidable in achieving the ultimate dream.

Some people speculate that The Pennsylvania State University was chosen as the academic home for the medical center because Mr. Hinkle was on their Board of Trustees. This is not entirely true. Dr. Walker, President of The Pennsylvania State University (TPSU), was approached by Mr. Hinkle, and others, in Hershey, PA on April 23, 1963 about an affiliation with TPSU. Mr. Hinkle was elected to the TPSU Board of Trustees on June 6, 1963, which was after an agreement had been made to affiliate, in principle, with the M. S. Hershey Foundation. A public announcement of the $50 million gift and proposed affiliation was made on August 23, 1963 (the formal affiliation agreement was signed by TPSU and the Trust August 27, 1963). Although there is no proof, it is thought that the President of the University, Dr. Eric Walker, "planted" Mr. Hinkle's nomination for TPSU Board of Trustees through one of the other trustees.

Mr. Hinkle had a very active role in the establishment of the medical center through his representation of the Hershey interests and as a member of TPSU Board of Trustees and TPSU Advisory Committee for the establishment of a medical center. In regard to the latter, he felt somewhat ill at ease serving with such renowned members of the scientific community. He often confided this privately to others and, reflecting his humble nature, refused to accept the $2500 honorarium offered for each meeting (although several meetings were envisioned, they actually met only once) and donated his travel reimbursement to the Trustee's Auxiliary Fund of TPSU. Mr. Hinkle was also a participant in major meetings concerning the medical center including those reviews requesting matching funds from the Federal Government for construction.

Mr. Hinkle's son was in medical school at the time of the initial medical center construction, and "boarded" his car in the garage behind Long Lane (a former Milton Hershey School student home and the initial administrative building for the medical center). Mr. Hinkle came out to Long Lane most Saturday mornings to start the car and sometimes take it for a drive. It also gave him a good opportunity to talk to me about what was going on and probably to figure out this first faculty appointment, a veterinarian (me).

An honorary society was formed for full Professors in the College of Medicine and named in Mr. Hinkle's honor, i.e., The Hinkle Society. He attended most meetings of the Society until his health declined. He was also a frequent visitor at many special lectures held in the medical center auditorium.

Gilbert Nurick

Born: November 23, 1906
Died: October 28, 1993
Education: A,B.(1928) The
Pennsylvania
State University
LL.B. (1931) Dickinson
School of Law
Positions: McNees, Wallace & Nurick
Senior Partner
Hershey Foods Corporation
Board of Directors

circa 1964

Mr. Nurick was a brilliant lawyer, very humble, and with very high ethical standards. He described himself as the son of immigrants who were poor, hard working, and very humble with high ethical standards. Every member of the family had to work, even the children as soon as they were able to walk, e.g. newspaper route, selling pretzels on the street, etc. He had a newspaper stand on a corner in Harrisburg, PA where people would buy their newspaper on their way to work. He was especially attracted to those men in suits with a briefcase on their way to the court house. When these men had a little extra time, they talked to him about what they were doing. He decided that he would like to be a lawyer, but education was out of the question. Because of very limited family finances, he quit school at age 14 and worked in a factory. Some of his school faculty persuaded him to return to school the following year. When he came back to high school, however, he took only commercial courses because he knew he would have to enter the labor market when he graduated. He was near the top of his class, and his principal told him that he HAD to go to college. Mr. Nurick argued that he had taken only commercial credits and had no money. The principal said that he would get him admitted, on a probationary basis, at Penn State. He went and found enough work to survive; washing dishes, tending furnaces, typing (thanks to his commercial courses in high school), etc. His father died right after his junior year in college. His plan, at that time, had been to graduate and teach in one of the Philadelphia schools and go to law school at night. Because of his father's death, he had to help his mother and sister in the family grocery store so he did his practice teaching in Harrisburg, PA, then returned to Penn State for his final semester and graduated. Since he still had to help in the grocery store and look after his mother and sister, he decided to enroll in the Dickinson School of Law.

As Mr. Nurick described it, he had the "good fortune" to graduate from law school at the depth of the Great Depression. Firms were laying off lawyers, not hiring them. However, he was hired as an associate by Mr. McNees at a salary of $50 per month - which was $50 more than anyone else was getting.

Although Mr. Nurick was married with 2 children, he joined the U. S. Navy in 1943; he felt that Hitler's war was his war too. After his time in the Navy he returned to Harrisburg, PA in 1946 and learned that Mr. McNees had had a heart attack. In Mr. Nurick's absence, Mr. McNees had been retained by the Hershey interests to handle labor relations. Mr. Nurick filled that gap, working with Mr. Sam Hinkle who, at that time, was the Plant Manager of The Hershey Chocolate Company. This resulted in a very cordial personal and professional relationship. Over time, Mr. Nurick's firm, more or less, became the general counsel for not only The Hershey Chocolate Company but also, the Milton Hershey School, the M. S. Hershey Trust, the M. S. Hershey Foundation, and the other Hershey interests. For corporate matters, the Hershey Chocolate Company also had, as their principal counsel, a well-known, prestigious New York law firm.

Mr. Nurick met Mr. Hershey on only one occasion; and it was adversarial. During construction of the community building the company that had the contract for elevators had subcontracted with another supplier for elevator doors. The elevator contractor went bankrupt and failed to pay the subcontractor for the doors. The subcontractor contacted Mr. Nurick who filed a mechanics lien against the building. Mr Nurick soon received a call saying that Mr. Hershey wanted to see him. Mr. Nurick met Mr. Hershey in Mr. Hershey's office and he was sitting there smoking a cigar with his personal lawyer, Mr. John E. Snyder, who also had a cigar, but unlighted. Mr. Hershey got right to the point and asked "Could you tell me why we should pay the bill twice? We already paid the elevator company." Mr. Nurick replied that the mechanics lien law was enacted to protect subcontractors not paid by the contractor. If Mr. Hershey had filed a notice or waiver of mechanics liens, the subcontractor could not have filed a lien. Mr. Hershey looked at his lawyer, who appeared uneasy, and said "Judge, why didn't we file it?" I'm not sure of the answer, but the bill was paid.

Mr. Nurick always gave substantial credit to a young lawyer in his firm, Mr. Jack Riggs, for all the research required for the *Cy Pres*. Unfortunately, he died an untimely death and did not live to see the fruits of his labors. All this research of background information, some of which included old English law, was used to prepare the Memorandum of Understanding and a Petition that led to the *Decree* establishing the medical center. Mr. Nurick was very proud of this achievement, and rightly so, and considered himself "… one of the multiple fathers of the medical center along with Arthur Whiteman, Sam Hinkle, John Hershey, and George Harrell."

John O. Hershey

Born: February 20, 1916
Died: February 20, 2006
Education: B. A. (1938) Taylor Univ
    M. A. (1943) Univ of Penn
    Ed.D. (1948) Univ of Penn
Positions: Milton Hershey School
    President
    Board of Managers,
    Chairman
    Hershey Estates
    Vice President
    Board of Directors
    Hershey Trust Company
    Assistant Vice President
    Board of Directors

circa 1964

Dr. John O. Hershey (no relation to Milton S. Hershey) was born and raised on a farm in Ohio. Dr. Hershey graduated from college at the end of the Great Depression. He and his wife took a position as house parents at the Milton Hershey School. In addition to being house parents to teenage boys, he was responsible for 180 acres of farmland and 36 dairy cows.

At the Milton Hershey School, Dr. Hershey quickly rose through the ranks from houseparent/farmer to teacher and guidance counselor, Dean of Students, Director of Enrollment & Student Personnel Services, Superintendent, and President. As part of his administrative duties, he became aware of the increasing income and decreasing expenditures of the Milton Hershey School, resulting in a rather large surplus of funds. Deciding that the School was their first priority, they undertook an intense, detailed survey, with expert advice, on how to improve their educational program and update all of their facilities. After completing a detailed internal program analysis of the institution, they brought in an external committee of consultants to review their plan in depth. The external committee accepted every one of their recommendations.

It was estimated that it would cost $50 million to implement this plan for expansion/renovation, leaving $50 million for some other purpose.

After the decision had been made to establish a medical center with the additional accumulated funds, Dr. Hershey was asked, by the M.S. Hershey Foundation, to serve as liaison (his official title was "Coordinator, Hershey Foundation Medical Center Committee) between the Trust and The Pennsylvania State University. His selection for this position was based on his administrative skills, experience in major construction projects, knowledge of Mr. Hershey's wishes, charisma, diplomacy, and ability to get things done. He was exemplary in this new, but additional, role.

Dr. Hershey occasionally attended the construction job meetings, usually when there was a problem. A contractor would say that they had been informed that a major piece of equipment would not be delivered on time; sometimes delayed by several months and, in one situation as much as one year late. Dr. Hershey made notes on the supplier, piece of equipment, original ship date, etc. He would then leave the room and the meeting continued. Dr. Hershey later returned to the meeting to announce that the piece of equipment in question would be delivered on time as originally scheduled. At the time, I thought that he was calling a Milton Hershey alumnus in the company responsible for the equipment because I knew that many of them had become very successful. Several years later, I asked him if he was using the Milton Hershey School connection. He said no, that he would call the contact person and ask if he could speak for the president of the company. If they said "no", he would ask to be transferred to some one who could speak for the president of the company. Dr. Hershey continued this line of inquiry until someone said "yes"; sometimes he would be transferred all the way to the president. Upon getting a "yes" answer, he would tell his story: "...I've got $50 million...to build a medical school and teaching hospital, and we are on a very tight schedule...if your company cannot deliver the equipment as originally scheduled, it will hold up the entire project." As I recall, this happened 6 or 8 times, and he was always successful in getting the original shipment date.

Dr. Hershey always paid attention to detail. I was impressed, when I met with him on the Milton Hershey School campus, that he appeared to know every student by name. He not only knew individual names, but he also knew how they were doing in school and sports, especially if they were doing well. Dr. Hershey was indeed a "people person." He liked people and relished working closely with them to help achieve common goals. He knew how to get things done expeditiously.

Eric A. Walker

Born: April 29, 1910
Died: February 20, 1995
Education: Harvard University
      B.S.- Electrical Engineering
      (1932)
      M.S.- Business
      Administration (1933)
      Sc.D.- (1935)
Position: The Pennsylvania State
      University
      President

circa 1964

Dr. Eric A. Walker was born in England, but raised in South Central Pennsylvania . He once described Mr. Sam Hinkle and himself as "poor boys" who grew up in the same geographical area and recognized the need for education. Dr. Walker was bright and an effective leader. While he was still a graduate student at Harvard, he was an instructor in mathematics at Tufts College. He remained at Tufts after graduation from Harvard, being promoted up the academic ladder at a very rapid rate, becoming Head of the Department of Electrical Engineering before assuming a similar appointment at the University of Connecticut. He was then recruited as Associate Director of the Harvard's Underwater Sound Laboratory. He was subsequently appointed Head, Department of Electrical Engineering and Director of TPSU Ordnance Research

Laboratory before becoming Dean of the College of Engineering and Architecture. He was appointed Vice President for Research and later that same year, in 1956, President of The Pennsylvania State University - at the age of 46. Upon his retirement from TPSU in 1970, he became Vice President of The Aluminum Company of America (Alcoa). His rapid rise in academia, multiple appointments in different parts of The Pennsylvania State University, and appointment as president of the university at a relatively young age, all attest to his scholarly ability, standing in the university, and leadership skills.

Dr. Walker was quite modest. He attributed his leadership success to an excellent staff, primarily Wil Kenworthy, McKay Donkin, and John Rackley. In addition to thinking a lot alike, they hunted, fished, hiked in the woods and socialized together. Dr. Walker's style of management was efficient. If someone needed a final decision from him, they would spell it out in a brief memo. If Dr. Walker approved the request, it came back with a circled W in green ink (referred to by many as the "green weenie"). Occasionally, he would ask for more information. No response meant "no". He believed in a prompt response to all requests, usually within 24 hours; if he was out of town, he would reply within 24 hours of his return. He had a similar approach to his Board of Trustees, and relied very heavily on his Executive Committee (Cappy Rowland, Walter Patchel and Charles Oakes). Items were essentially for confirmation by the time they reached the full Board of Trustees. In addition to his heavy workload with the university, he also found time to work as a consultant, be a member of national professional and educational organizations, where he often served in leadership roles. He received numerous awards and honorary degrees.

The Commonwealth Campus System of TPSU was developed under the leadership of Dr. Milton Eisenhower, his predecessor as President of The Pennsylvania State University. Dr. Walker continued that growth. Dr. Eisenhower transformed the institution from the Pennsylvania State College to The Pennsylvania State University (1953). This expansion, under the leadership of both Presidents Eisenhower and Walker provided unique educational opportunities to the citizens of the commonwealth, along with the number of other, high quality, smaller liberal arts colleges. However, Dr Walker believed that Penn State would never be a "true university" without law and medical schools.

He almost reached an affiliation with the Dickinson School of Law when the negotiations suddenly "blew up" in the early 1960's (Dr. Walker would not elaborate because he said that it was a "sensitive matter" but the Dickinson School of Law did later affiliate with The Pennsylvania State University in 1997). The issue of a medical school was more problematic. Dr Walker concluded that the Commonwealth had an oversupply of medical schools compared to surrounding states (which at that time had none or only one) and that the Commonwealth was, in effect, subsidizing the other states by training their physicians. Furthermore, he was very politically astute, and knew that another medical school would have to be at the expense of existing programs. At that time, the university's funding was approximately 1/3 for resident instruction, 1/3 for continuing education, and 1/3 for research. He was not about to invoke the ire of his faculty by encroaching on those funds. He then attempted to forge a formal affiliation with Jefferson Medical College, and was about to do so when the Hershey money for a medical center became available.

Dr. Walker was also cautious about making decisions that could have a subsequent, unfavorable impact. He liked to replay the university's origin as a land grant institution. This was made possible by the Morrill Land Grant Act (1862). This was a Federal Act that, in essence, said the United States should have colleges that were practical. The Act did not say that you can't teach liberal arts but you HAD to teach agriculture and you HAD to teach mechanical arts. The traditional educational programs, at that time, were for teachers, ministers, doctors and lawyers. But the country had a dire need for engineers and surveyors, canal builders, railroad builders, etc. They later passed another bill stating that you must do research in agriculture and mechanical arts. The programs were funded by providing approximately one million acres of Federal land and matching funds from each state. If the land was available in a state, they took it for their own land grant university; if not, they took it from an unseeded state in the West. Pennsylvania did not have enough Federal land so they took their share, one million acres, in Utah and sold it for 40 cents an acre, or slightly less than ½ million dollars and the Commonwealth made it up to 1 million dollars. Ninety seven years later, uranium was discovered on this land in Utah!

George T. Harrell

Born: June 16, 1908
Died: August 26, 1999
Education: A.B. (1932) Duke
University
M.D. (1936) Duke University
Position: The Pennsylvania State Univ.
Dean, College of Medicine
Vice President for Health
Affairs

circa 1964

Dr. George T. Harrell, the founding Dean of The Milton S. Hershey Medical Center, was humble and modest, a hard worker, and also a visionary, intelligent, resourceful educator.

Dr. Harrell's career was quite remarkable, given that he never thought that he would go to college, much less medical school because of limited financial means. He was born in Washington, D.C. where his father was a successful merchant, running a family shoe store. His mother was quite ill (later determined to be tuberculosis). On one occasion, she was sent to Ashville, NC to recuperate but her health continued to decline after she returned home. His father decided to move the family to the Ashville, NC area hoping to improve his wife's health. After moving, his father decided to start a specialty meats store and promptly went broke. Dr. Harrell was an excellent student in high school and particularly enjoyed chemistry. He wrote a senior paper on chemistry in the automobile industry, actually contacting the major automobile companies for information. Most of them responded. After graduation from high school, since he had no funds for college, he started a sports store, selling equipment, re-stringing tennis racquets, etc. After a few years, he took advantage of an unexpected opportunity to sell the business and go to college. Since he was not yet 21, he had to have a guardian for his money (according to the law his father could not serve in that role). Over Dr. Harrell's objections, his guardian put the money into several banks, all of which failed during the Great Depression after his freshman year at Duke University. Dr. Harrell wrote to Duke University saying that he could not return because of his financial situation. Since he had been an excellent student and a natural student leader, they encouraged him to return and helped him to find jobs in the bookstore and library. He returned to Duke University, and envisioned an ultimate career in the pharmaceutical industry combining his interests in science and economics. During that time Duke University was building a new medical school and the founding dean, Dr. Davison, was a frequent visitor in both the bookstore and library. It is interesting to note that Dr. Davison had little, or no, input in the design of the medical school. His job was to recruit a faculty and plan a curriculum. When the building was finished, he was given the keys to the building and told to do with it what he could. Back to Dr. Harrell's undergraduate education, he took a course in physiology and thoroughly enjoyed it. He talked to Dr. Davison about this, and Dr. Davison suggested that he think about medical school; something that he had never considered because of financial limitations. Dr Davison assisted him in becoming the night manager of the bookstore on the men's campus (he had a similar position on the women's campus). They also asked him to open a haberdashery during the summer months, which further increased his income. Dr. Davison also had an arrangement with two elderly, unmarried school teachers who wanted someone to live in their house for protection. Dr. Harrell did not recall applying for medical school; he just went! After his second year in medical school, he visited the Dean, saying that he would simply not have the time to continue his working arrangements and carry out his responsibilities on the wards. Dr. Davison arranged for him to be the night man in the medical school library instead of working in the bookstore.

As Dr. Harrell was finishing his medical school studies, he applied for an internship in internal medicine. He wanted to become a diagnostician. Actually, there was little else that one could to do then because almost no effective drug therapy existed for any of the major diseases. He spent the summer between his junior and senior years working in pathology. From his work in the library, Dr. Harrell realized that Sir William Osler was the outstanding physician at the turn of the century, and his career was based, mainly, on his experience in pathology. After his first year as a resident in medicine, Dr. Harrell applied to work as a student volunteer in pathology during the summer, continuing his night job in the library. At the end of his internship, he was one of two being considered for the position of chief resident. The wife of the other candidate was a secretary in the anatomy department and the school needed her. Dr. Harrell thought about this situation, and made a proposition to his chief that he go back to pathology for a year to better prepare for his clinical experience. His chief agreed. However, in the middle of the year, he got a call from the head of medicine telling him that he was to report to the City Memorial Hospital in Winston-Salem, NC to cover for the pathologist who had became ill. He believed that he had no business doing this as an assistant resident and after only six months of formal training in pathology. But he went and decided that if he could make it, he really wanted to teach. He quickly organized clinical pathology and autopsy conferences for local physicians in the community. He lived in the hospital and quickly found that they had no bacteriology laboratory. He worked to develop that capability; doing most of it himself. Word of his teaching filtered back to Duke University and the head of pathology asked him to take over his section of the pathology course, since he was engaged in writing a book. Dr Harrell readily agreed to do so, if he could teach in his own way. That included using patients and laboratory studies to correlate with the disease process. He encouraged the students to talk to patients, try to determine what parts of the body might be affected, what physiologic and clinical changes could be detected and what laboratory studies (most of which they had to do themselves) could be used to confirm or exclude a possible diagnosis. It was an immediate success.

He frequently presented his teaching, laboratory, and research data at Duke University conferences. After one presentation, the dean of the faculty at the Bowman Gray School of Medicine, Wake Forest University in Winston-Salem, NC came up and introduced himself. He said that they now had a two year medical school (which required that the students transfer to another medical school for their last two years) but were in the process of expanding it to 4 years; would Dr. Harrell like to be a part of it? Thus, he became the first clinical faculty appointment to the new Bowman Gray School of Medicine. He told the dean, who was a pathologist, that he wanted to continue some of his teaching experiences that he had done at Duke University. The dean readily agreed. Since there were no clinical students yet, he started introducing the students in the basic science years to patients. He impressed on them that if something doesn't fit a disease process, it may be behavioral or a functional overlay. He designed several teaching laboratories using live (but anesthetized) animals to demonstrate blood flow, physiologic changes, and super vital stains to demonstrate structures in the kidneys and liver. The students were excited to see these changes in living tissue instead of dead, preserved tissue slides.

Since the Bowman Gray Medical School was started in the North Carolina Baptist Hospital, they had no teaching facilities in the beginning and every thing had to be improvised. However, Dr. Harrell persisted and soon he was doing all of the correlation teaching. He also developed a research program on Rocky Mountain Spotted Fever (RMSF). One of his papers on that subject was later cited as a Citation Classic in Medicine. He was one of the first to use a new drug, aureomycin, to treat RMSF. Very quickly, RMSF turned from being a disease of almost certain mortality to one of quick recovery.

Dr. Harrell continued his educational experiments and studies on infectious diseases, and preparing exhibits for national meetings. However, he was seeing very few patients which meant a very low income. One of the wealthy families in Winston-Salem heard about this and approached the dean of the medical school about setting up a permanent endowment, the income of which would be used to supplement Dr. Harrell's salary. The dean agreed, which raised his income to $7,500 a year – his highest salary while he was in Winston-Salem. The dean interpreted this to mean that Dr. Harrell would be a full-time laboratory researcher. Dr. Harrell strongly disagreed because he wanted to be a clinician, educator AND researcher, combining all three. He decided then that he would leave when the right opportunity came along.

By coincidence, the University of Florida was planning to build a medical school. The architect had heard about Dr. Harrell's teaching experiences. The president at the University of Florida had also heard about Dr. Harrell's exhibits and presentations on correlation teaching. The president offered Dr. Harrell the deanship of the new school. Dr. Harrell agreed to accept if he could continue his clinical correlation studies. The president agreed and suggested that, since it would be two years before there would be a building to occupy, he and the architect go around and visit newer medical schools. Dr. Harrell and the architect spent the next year visiting all schools that had been built since World War II. As they toured these buildings, Dr. Harrell discussed what they were attempting, what works, and what does not. At night they would return to their hotel and review all the day's new information. By the time of his formal appointment as the new dean, he and the architect already had a sketch for the new building. He also used this time to solidify his thoughts on including family and community medicine, behavioral science, and humanities into the new curriculum. Everything was going great. He had an excellent rapport with the president of the university who actively supported his plans. Unfortunately, the president suddenly died a few months after Dr. Harrell's appointment. The president was succeeded by his vice president who had made it very clear that he had not wanted a medical school and disagreed with Dr. Harrell's innovative educational plans.

Soon thereafter, Dr. Walker, President of The Pennsylvania State University asked Dr. Harrell to come to talk to him, some of his Trustees, the Hershey people and some of the Advisory Committee (appointed by Dr. Walker to plan for a medical center) about how a university went about planning for a medical school. Dr. Harrell thought that he was going merely as a consultant (without a fee) which he frequently did for other schools because he thought, as a dean, he had an obligation to do so. However, it appears, retrospectively, that Dr. Walker was using this as a ploy to size him up as a potential dean. Dr. Harrell was excused from the meeting along with the university lawyer and, after a short discussion, it was unanimously agreed that this was "the man".

William Christensen

Born: April 17, 1917
Died:
Education: B.S., Civil Engineering (1939)
Massachusetts Institute of
Technology

<no image available>

Position: Hershey Chocolate Corporation
Manager, Construction
Manager, Project Engineering

William Christensen started his career with a construction firm in New York City (Turner Construction Company). After two years with this company, he spent another two years with the War Department, U. S. Engineers in the New Orleans District as a civil engineer on flood control, rivers, and harbors.

In 1943, Mr. Christensen enlisted in the U.S. Navy, as an officer in a construction battalion, then as an operating officer in the Central Pacific for harbor development and later, as a member of the famed Seabees in forward areas.

After World War II, Mr. Christensen worked for a major construction corporation, (The Nicholson Company, Inc) rising through the ranks of Job Engineer, Superintendent and, ultimately, Project Manager, He worked on 30 different projects, some simultaneously, from the East Coast to the West Coast. He and his family moved 26 times in 25 years. One of his projects was as Construction Superintendent for construction of silos for Hershey Chocolate Company for storing cocoa beans, still a landmark in Central Pennsylvania. It was a major logistical feat requiring the continuous pouring of concrete, once each silo was started.

It was fortuitous that, after completing a job in California, he and his wife were driving to their home in New Jersey when they noticed a highway sign that said "Hershey". On the spur of the moment, they decided to take a detour to see an old friend, Lou Smith, who was Hershey Chocolate Company's chief engineer. They had become close friends during construction of the silos, and remained so. Within a few days, Mr. Christensen was being interviewed by the M. S. Hershey Foundation for the job as Construction Manager of The Milton S.

Hershey Medical Center. Bill was both pleased and excited because of the challenge and it felt like they were coming home. They admired the people in the Hershey interests and Central Pennsylvania – and they were tired of moving.

Mr. Christensen's specific instructions from Dr. John Hershey/ Hershey Foundation were to "… conduct continuous construction, implementing the policies of the M. S. Hershey Foundation and The Pennsylvania State University and to make day-by-day, on site decisions to help achieve the design prepared by the architects and engineers." Bill stated that Dr Hershey told him " fast answers are essential if a tight schedule is to be met."

Mr. Christensen wished that he had been involved earlier in the project, especially in dealing with construction aspects of the job. Nevertheless, because of his expertise in managing and supervising construction, the project became a reality.

C. Max Lang

Born: December 29, 1937
Education: University of Illinois
    B.S. (1959)
    D.V.M. (1961)
Position: The Pennsylvania State
    University
        George T Harrell Professor
        &Founding Chair,
        Department of
        Comparative Medicine

circa 1966

The author, Dr. C. Max Lang, was born and raised on a farm in Illinois. After receiving his Doctor of Veterinary Medicine degree, and facing the draft, he enlisted in the U.S. Army and was assigned to the Walter Reed Army Institute of Research in Washington, D.C.. This was his first exposure to research and Laboratory Animal Medicine. In addition to his army responsibilities, he was the veterinarian for President Kennedy's dogs, Charlie and Pushinka (Pushinka was the offspring of the first dog sent into space by the U.S.S.R. and a gift from Premier Khrushchev to President Kennedy), pets of various Cabinet Officers, and pets of military officers with one or more "stars" on their shoulders. Associating with these people and their pets was an education in itself.

After completing his military obligation, Dr. Lang enrolled in a postdoctoral program at Wake Forest University for research training and training in the specialty of Laboratory Animal Medicine. He was the first faculty member appointed by the founding dean of the College of Medicine in June, 1966. At that time Hershey was the only medical school, perhaps in the world, that was ½ dean and ½ veterinarian – it has never been so good since!

One may question why a veterinarian was the first faculty appointment to a new medical school. That question was certainly asked by both Dr. Walker and Mr. Hinkle. Dr. Harrell pointed out to both that he realized that he would be competing with several new medical schools (14 in that era) as well as existing ones for the best faculty. Thus, he thought that a first-rate animal research facility would be a major recruiting aid. The same questions were asked when he told them that the Animal Research Farm would be one of the first buildings completed (number two, after the steam plant). His answer was the same, i.e. visible evidence of his commitment to teaching and research. On a more practical matter, he was requesting construction funds from the federal government for the Animal Research Farm, and having a director of the new facility at the time of the site visit (April, 1966) was very important.

Upon Dr. Lang's arrival in Hershey, there were no buildings and no research animals, so Dr. Harrell asked him to serve as a liaison between his office and construction. Dr. Lang attended the construction job meetings and designed the research laboratories in the basic science and clinical science wings. He had no experience in designing research and teaching laboratories and none of the faculty had been hired, but Dr. Harrell was an excellent mentor.

Dr. Lang developed a strong Department of Comparative Medicine emphasizing quality animal care, research, and teaching (Dr. Lang and two of his former students have received the prestigious Charles River Prize, given annually, in recognition of distinguished contributions to laboratory animal science; no other training program has received this number of Charles River Prizes). Students were constantly reminded that they had both a moral and scientific responsibility to provide the highest level of care to the animals. Every animal was seen every day, 365 days a year, by a veterinarian; something never previously achieved by an HMO (Health Maintenance Organization.) for humans.

Dr. Lang developed an active research program receiving over $11 million, as principal investigator, in peer-reviewed research funding. His educational and research activities resulted in more than 150 invited lectures in this country and abroad, invited as a Visiting Professor to 25 national and international universities, and publishing 3 books and 178 scientific articles in peer-reviewed publications. He served on more than 25 Federal Government scientific panels and committees. He also served on numerous University and College committees.

His career exemplifies what can become possible in a fertile and collegial environment.

Summary of People

A review of the events and people who were instrumental in building The Milton S. Hershey Medical Center, indeed, reflects an impossible dream i.e.:

Transfer of funds: from one of the most tightly written wills,

Matching Federal funds for a project that would not be owned by the university and on land that would not be owned by the university,

An orphan who came to the Milton Hershey School because he was caught playing in the Susquehanna River, and had planned to be a house painter,

An astute businessman who had no experience in medical schools,

A skilled lawyer who had not planned to go to law school because of financial limitations,

A charismatic administrator,

A dean who did not think that college was possible, much less medical school,

A highly qualified construction engineer who just happened to take a detour on his way from California to New Jersey.

These events may be serendipity but the people were characterized by humility, an ethic of hard work, and a commitment to the ideals of Milton Hershey. Yes, it was an Impossible Dream.

Chapter 2 – Accumulation of Money

Milton Hershey built a chocolate factory, made a lot of money, started a home for orphan boys, built a model community for his employees, and, because they still had too much money, his successors built a medical center. Sounds fantastic, and this is what a lot of people believe. Unfortunately, it was not that simple, nor completely true. It does provide a nice time line, but it does not address the difficulties, uncertainties, frustrations, commitment, or hard work in this achievement; success was due to an unusual combination of the right people, at the right time, and in the right place.

It is true that Milton Hershey was a successful candy manufacturer. But he achieved this success after several abysmal business failures. Only then did he establish a very successful caramel candy business in Lancaster, PA for which he had no formal training, little experience, and very little formal education (he left school after the fourth grade, and then only after attending eight different country schools). He is reported to have sold his caramel candy business for $1 million. Unlike many of his peers of that era, he did not take the money and retire to a life of luxury. Instead, he gambled all of his money to pursue his dream of making chocolate. He not only spent all his money, but he had to borrow more to complete his chocolate factory built in the middle of a corn field. Despite a lack of education and marketing training, he succeeded.

As his financial resources grew, Mr. Hershey spent his money to help others: a model community (definitely not a factory town) for his employees and a home for orphan boys.

One of his early admissions to the boys home, Arthur R. Whiteman, went on to become a financial wizard, and a person who deeply revered Mr. Hershey. He was appointed to the boards of the Hershey Trust Company, Milton Hershey School, and M. S. Hershey Foundation at an early age and these experiences, plus his working relationship with Milton Hershey, gave him a unique insight into the moneys available and Mr. Hershey's wishes.

Complementing the role of Mr. Whiteman was Mr. Hershey's appointment of Samuel F. Hinkle as Chief Chemist for the Hershey Chocolate Company. In this position, he worked very closely with Mr. Hershey for the last 21 years of his life. Mr. Hinkle also became reasonably familiar with Mr. Hershey's philosophies "without the need to become a hero-worshiper." Mr. Hinkle also became very knowledgeable about Mr. Hershey's interest in education since his own schooling was so meager. Mr. Hershey also had a strong attraction to new and better remedies for relieving human suffering, probably because of the illness and untimely death of his wife, Kitty, although he seldom mentioned her years of degenerating illness for which he could find no cure. Because of his working relationship with Mr. Hershey and appointment to several of the Hershey boards, Mr. Hinkle became aware of the increasing surplus of funds.

Why were funds accumulating in excess of expenses for the School? The answer is multifaceted. Enrollment declined dramatically during World War II. Rationing, because of war led to problems in obtaining clothing, food, gasoline, tires, etc. Many of the students were living on farms scattered around the township and items required for transportation were a real hardship. This coincided with a decrease in the number of available orphans. Due to the availability of social welfare funds and decreasing mortality of young parents, the combination of this with war rationing caused enrollment in the Milton Hershey School to drop below 700 from a high of over 1000 students. Several changes had been made to increase enrollment: extend the age eligibility from 4 to 8 years of age to 4 to 14, include orphans who were motherless and/or fatherless, and change the name from the Hershey Industrial School (thought to suggest that it was some type of a reformatory) to the Milton Hershey School to remove any stigma in recruiting students. These efforts were further enhanced by a national recruiting campaign, including touring Glee Club performances, and media events. In all these efforts, there was no mention of the School being the recipient of income from the chocolate factory; they did not want any inference of using orphans to sell chocolate. As expenses of the School continued to decline, the Hershey Chocolate Company continued to prosper due to excellent, conservative management – and largely without advertising. This success in business was accomplished, in part no doubt, by including a specially designed Hershey bar (D ration) in the GI rations and distribution of Hershey candy to war-ravaged children; thus, introducing thousands and thousands of people to Hershey Chocolate.

The issue of accumulating funds was discussed by the Board of the Hershey Trust Company on several occasions but no action was taken. There had already been reports in the popular press about the size of some of the well-known trusts in the U. S. and whether these trusts should retain their tax exempt status. The Hershey Trust board chairman, Mr. P. A. Staples, died suddenly in July, 1956 and the trustees had not reached any agreement on how to use these surplus funds.

Mr. John A. Sollenberger, successor chair of the trust, and some of the older members of the group had several, but rather infrequent, discussions about future actions to be taken. But, no actions were taken, although all agreed that the Milton Hershey School – education of the boys, their living conditions, the physical plant and, most important of all, the philosophies on the rearing of orphan boys to the status of upright American manhood was their first priority.

Mr. Hinkle was "...completely convinced that if Mr. Hershey could have been consulted, he would have approved heartily the proposition of dedicating any surplus funds, which might accrue through the years, to education in the healing arts, so long as his prime objective of caring for poor, orphan boys was fully assured. Since another trust established by Mr. Hershey (The M. S. Hershey Foundation) was devoted to educational purposes in Derry Township, Dauphin County, Pennsylvania, the obvious solution lay in the establishment of a medical school and teaching hospital in the Hershey area."

The trustees of the Trust began to concentrate their thinking on the continuing growth in the size of the trust and what action should be taken in relation to the overall problem. Mr Sollenberger, the chair, asked the trustees, as individuals, to submit their thoughts in writing. Mr. Hinkle wrote:

> "The first order of business is to get our present system in the best of order...,

> No time should be lost in launching and coordinating a program of this type...,

If we were to ask the court's permission for trust modification…to…admit boys from broken homes for example, it seems that we immediately would be inviting criticism of our methods…and in no time our worst fears of 'The line forming on the right' would be realities. It appears to me that there is a way to avoid this…,

It seems to me that a first-rate medical school, including an outstanding hospital, provides the perfect answer in our situation…As I think about it, it seems that all of our efforts in acquiring land and developing Derry Township, and all of our accumulation of trust funds through these years, have been pointing towards this one great opportunity to revere and perpetuate Mr. Hershey's name in a way that will bring credit to his memory and great satisfaction to us all."

Mr. Hinkle appended his own paper, "Thoughts for Improving Milton Hershey School" (copy not available). The letter and appendix were never acknowledged by Mr. Sollenberger, nor presented to the trustees. The matter of a medical school was superseded by implementation of plans for the fiftieth (1909 –1959) anniversary of the Milton Hershey School.

The Trustees appointed an "Anniversary Evaluation Committee" consisting of the best individuals they could find in the field of child care. It was chaired by Dr. Leonard W. Mayo, Executive Director of the Association for the Aid of Crippled Children, NYC, and assisted by Dr. Frederick Allen (a psychiatrist for the Philadelphia school district) and Miss Helen C. Hubbell (a retired employee of the Pennsylvania Department of Health and Welfare).

The Anniversary Evaluation Committee reviewed all of the programs and projections including recommendations made by the Trust and School. One conclusion was, given the size and type of the community, and considering the nature of the school, they should not expand the enrollment beyond 1600 students. The School presented the trustees and evaluation committee with financial projections, with cushions for inflation and contingencies, to implement all of the recommendations and concluded that they would still have $50 million remaining. That left the question of what to do with the remaining money.

Mr. Sollenberger retired on June 28, 1962 and was replaced by Mr. Whiteman as Chair of the Board of Trustees of the Hershey Trust Company. Within a few weeks, Messrs Whiteman and Hinkle reactivated the medical school project and, without any adverse opinions from any of the other trustees, inaugurated discussions with their legal advisors concerning the practical issues of the project.

Thus, the "money trail" was:

June, 1905	The chocolate factory is opened and, after a few years, became profitable.
Nov 15, 1909	"School Trust" established for the Hershey Industrial School (later changed to the Milton Hershey School, Dec 17, 1951).
1914	Mr. Hershey built, and donated the M. S. Hershey Consolidated School to Derry Township.
1915	Mr. Hershey built, and donated the Derry Township Junior-Senior School to Derry Township.
1918	Mr. Hershey gave the bulk of his assets to the School Trust in the form of capital stock in the Hershey Chocolate Company . (the only other contributions to this trust were Mr. Hershey's residual assets of $43,250; residual residence of Mr. John E. Snyder, Mr. Hershey's lawyer, appraised at $30,000; and residual residence of Mary Amos, relationship unknown to author, appraised at $2,500.

1933	The School Trust was enlarged and modified to permit current and accumulated income then being earned and held by the School Trust to be more fully spent for charitable purposes.
Dec 5, 1935	Established the M. S. Hershey Foundation Trust to support educational activities in Derry Township, Dauphin County, Pennsylvania (The Hershey Trust Company was named as the Trustee for the School Trust and the Hershey Foundation).
1938	Mr. Hershey successfully negotiated with the Derry Township School Board to build the Hershey Junior College.
Aug 23, 1963	The Pennsylvania Orphan's Court authorized the transfer of $50 million from the accumulated income fund of the Milton Hershey School Trust to the M. S. Hershey Foundation for the purpose of establishing a medical school to be located in Derry Township, Pennsylvania.

In the 1930's Mr. Hershey initiated the sale of his Cuban sugar plantations (17 in all, encompassing over 10,000 acres). Because of WW II, the sale of these lands to the Cuban-American Sugar Company was not completed until 1946, the year after Mr. Hershey's death. There are several stories that Mr. Hershey used the money from the land sale to finance many of the community building projects to avoid paying huge sums in U. S. taxes. However, many of the building projects were completed in the 1930's.

Chapter 3 – Legal Proceedings

The money was available to establish a medical school and teaching hospital. The. next step towards establishing The Milton S. Hershey Medical Center was almost an insurmountable hurdle, i.e., the legal aspects of the Trust. Mr. Hershey's Deed of Trust was believed, by several legal experts, to be very restrictive in its interpretation of how the funds could be spent. Mr. Hinkle, president of the Hershey Chocolate Company and a member of the various Hershey boards, initially consulted a well-known and prestigious New York City law firm that provided legal counsel on corporate matters for the Hershey Chocolate Company on how to proceed in transferring the money from one trust to another in a way that was believed to be consistent with Mr. Hershey's wishes. This law firm studied the issue, conducted research on related issues, and reviewed the plan for transferring the assets. After much investigation and review, they submitted a very definite opinion, very scholarly, and concluded that it could not be done. Mr. Hinkle then turned to his friend, Mr. Gilbert Nurick, whose firm was increasingly handling legal matters for the Hershey interests. Mr. Nurick saw this as a challenge; he never believed in being a "veto lawyer." He told Mr. Hinkle "…if you don't try it, then you don't know it can't be done. If you do try it, you take a hell of a risk, letting the world know you've got $50 million to donate to charity, and you're going to have a lot of people banging on your door for it."

During this period of time there was a lot of discussion about the use of the surplus funds. The priority was oriented towards a medical school but what if $50 million was too much to achieve this goal? Strange as it may seem, this was a real concern at one time. Some of the board members of the trust thought that they should expand the Hershey Junior College into a four year college. This was based on the fact that Mr. Hershey had, in the 1930's, inquired whether the Lebanon Valley College would want to move their campus from Annville, PA to Hershey; but they did not want to give up their religious affiliation. There was some dissension among the Hershey people about expanding the Hershey Junior College into a four year college because a lot of people who did not work for the Hershey interests had moved into Derry Township solely for the purpose of the free tuition. This, in turn, caused the cost of real estate to significantly go up in value (something that they thought would have infuriated Mr. Hershey; Mr. Harold Mohler, successor to Mr. Hinkle as president of the Hershey Chocolate Company, told me that "...he (Mr. Hershey) would have knocked that off...because if there was anything he detested was somebody not joining in the spirit of something...". They considered other educational ventures, e.g., a technical school because of Mr. Hershey's interest in vocational training. However, because of their distaste of people taking advantage of "free" benefits, they came to the realization that they did not have the infrastructure for these ventures. Nevertheless, the Hershey Junior College would have to close. Even though it had a high quality program and its credits were readily accepted by other colleges and universities, it was limited in scope, and it would require massive renovations to meet new building codes for educational purposes.

Cy Pres

Mr. Nurick accepted the challenge posed by Mr. Hinkle to transfer funds from the trust to establish a medical school, and embarked on an arduous, in-depth analysis of the issues and charted a course of action. This course of action involved several phases, referred to as the doctrine of *Cy Pres*. *Cy Pres* is a noun, and a legal term used to refer to a process or rule to accomplish an objective, i.e., "a rule providing for the interpretation of instruments in equity as nearly as possible in conformity to the intention of the testator when literal construction is illegal, impracticable, or impossible (Webster)".

The next step in the *Cy Pres* was to prepare a Factual Statement for review by the Attorney General of Pennsylvania, who represents the interests of the citizens of the Commonwealth.

Statement

The Statement (a seven page document) starts by "On November 15, 1909, Milton S. Hershey. founder of the Hershey Chocolate Company, executed a deed of trust for the establishment of a permanent institution for the residence and education of poor orphan boys." A key word is *permanent*, because it emphasizes the need for funds to be used in perpetuity. At a time of surplus funds, how do you know when "enough is enough"? You cannot continue to accumulate surplus funds indefinitely because of Federal tax laws governing the tax-exempt status of a trust.

At the time of this Statement (May 8, 1963) "...there were 1,171 students enrolled in the school and, in accordance with Mr. Hershey's expressed wishes, there was a special emphasis on vocational and technical training for qualified students."

The Statement also emphasized "...for several years, the Trustees and Managers of the School had given very serious consideration to the use of a portion of the accumulated funds for some project which would be consonant with Mr. Hershey's general charitable purposes and, at the same time, would meet a critical public need...request court approval to establish a medical school in Derry Township, which is located in the metropolitan Harrisburg area." It goes on to say "...anticipates that approximately $25,000,000 will be required to construct and equip a thoroughly modern and efficient medical school and teaching hospital... (and)...sufficient...annual payments...(towards the)...cost of operating the new institution." Unfortunately, these estimated costs, no matter how well intended, would lead to problems in the future.

The Statement also emphasized "...Mr. Hershey's charitable interests were concentrated in the field of education and particularly as it related to institutions or establishments in Derry Township...Milton Hershey School...M. S. Hershey Foundation (established Sept 3, 1910 and Dec 5, 1935 respectively)...for the establishment and maintenance of educational institutions in Derry Township as well as support...the improvement and elevation of the standard of education." These phrases became the basis for dictating that funds from his Deed of Trust had to be spent for education and in Derry Township.

The Statement reiterated "In 1920 there were an estimated 6.4 million orphaned children (16 percent of the child population under 18) compared with 2.9 million in 1961 (4 percent of the same population)... the decline in the number of full orphans from 750,000 in 1920 to 55,000 in 1961...(was due, in part to a) substantial reduction in mortality rates for both men and women...in the United States....in

Dec 1960, seven out of ten paternal orphans were supported at least in part by benefits based on the deceased father's earning record."

The second issue addressed in the Statement was the critical need for doctors. The Statement referenced a report by the U. S. Surgeon General that stated: "...in order to maintain the current (1959) ratio of physicians to population (141 per 100,000), the nation would require 330,000 physicians by 1975, at a rate of 11,000 graduates per year or almost a 50 percent increase in output." This report also recommended that, wherever possible, the medical school should be a part of a university and supplemented with a teaching hospital. It should be noted that Dr. George T. Harrell, the founding dean of The Milton S. Hershey Medical Center, was a member of the committee that wrote this report for the Surgeon General. Because a number of states had no medical school, and Pennsylvania had six, it was believed that the possibility of receiving Federal aid for another medical school in Pennsylvania was "...most remote."

Mr. Nurick submitted the Statement to the Attorney General, Walter Allessandroni, in the form of a brief to avoid the need for a public notice or hearing. Mr. Allessandroni accepted the Statement and said "Look, leave the papers here. We'll review them, study them, and the idea fascinates me. But, I can do only what the law permits me to do. I have to be convinced." He turned the papers over to his Chief Deputy, Edward Friedman, for further review. After several weeks and additional meetings, the Attorney General was convinced that it was legal and that he would officially concur. The papers were then presented to Judge Lee Swope, President Judge of the Orphan's Court which, among other duties, had jurisdiction over the Milton Hershey School. Judge Swope was a lawyer and had been head of the Corporate Bureau in the Department of State for Pennsylvania before going onto the bench. He had run on the Democratic ticket and won. Democrats never won in Dauphin County in those days but he won because so many people disliked his opponent. Mr. Nurick described Judge Swope as an "...able and outstanding jurist, and sees people instead of just principles and words". Mr. Nurick assured Judge Swope that the Attorney General was in agreement with the plan and had authorized him to submit it to the Judge without the Attorney General or his deputy being present. Judge Swope received the papers that covered every angle, including the right to consider without public notice and the right to sign it in his chambers. Judge Swope said: "… the idea excites me but I've got to feel I can do legally what you're asking me to do." After several weeks, Judge Swope called Mr. Nurick and said "I think that I can go for it." Mr. Nurick then met with the Hon. William Scranton, Governor of Pennsylvania. Although it was mainly a courtesy call, the Governor immediately endorsed the plan.

This entire process had been done entirely in secret. This may have been made possible, in part, by the introduction of a bill in the General Assembly of the Commonwealth of Pennsylvania "…to make an appropriation ($3.5 million) to the Board of Trustees of Pennsylvania State University for a medical school in Harrisburg, Pennsylvania, House Bill 371, February 25, 1963." Thus, in the case of a leak, people would automatically think that they were referring to this bill, which probably had no chance of being passed, and ignore any related comments.

Petition

The Petition (a 34 page document) for a *Cy Pres* Award of Portion of Accumulated funds was prepared for, and submitted to, the President Judge of the Orphans Court of Dauphin County, Lee F. Swope, and dated July, 1963. The Petition reviews the history of the Milton Hershey School and provides a description of the "School Trust" which was filed Nov 15, 1909 for the purpose of "…founding and endowing in perpetuity…for the purpose of…maintenance, education and training of orphan boys…" Pursuant to the terms of the School Trust, the School was established September 3, 1910 under the name of The Hershey Industrial School, later changed to the Milton Hershey School on Dec 17, 1951. A modification of the Trust was requested Oct 27, 1933 to: (1) change the age for admission to the school from between the ages of four and eight years, to the ages between four to fourteen years; (2) admit boys whose mothers were deceased, even though their fathers were still living.

The Petition states that Mr. Hershey transferred sums of money, securities and other personal property to the Hershey Trust Company, as trustee, as gifts for the endowment of the School, It also noted that Mr. Hershey's estate at the time of his death consisted of 345 shares of the Hershey Trust Company, having an aggregate appraised value of $43,250.

The Petition reviews all of the school property (in a summary format), the current status of buildings, including recent and planned renovations; planned new construction; current and planned staffing; enrollment patterns; operating income and expenditures; and projections for the future in all categories.

Mr. Hershey established the M. S. Hershey Foundation Dec 5, 1935 for the purposes of establishment and maintenance of educational facilities in Derry Township, PA, support of the public schools of Derry Township, PA, and the vocational, cultural or professional education of any resident of Derry Township, PA. The Petition proposes the transfer of $50 million of the surplus funds from the School Trust to the Foundation for the purpose of establishing a medical school.

Memorandum

The Memorandum is 97 pages in length and provides the background for the *Cy Pres* Petition. It cites 76 legal cases, most of which involved bequests for specific projects that could no longer be achieved, e.g., for expansion of a building or church that merged or ceased to function before the funds could be expended, insufficient funds for the intended project, or attempts of heirs or organizations to preempt the wishes of the donor.

The Memorandum was divided into sections: The Factual Background (basically a repeat/summary of the Petition), The Applicable Law, and Conclusions. In addition to the legal cases cited, it included a review of applicable statutes and rules (going back to 1855), and miscellaneous authorities

Decree

The two page Decree was signed by Judge Lee F. Swope on August 23, 1963, authorizing the transfer of $50 million in assets from the School Trust to the M. S. Hershey Foundation for the purpose of establishing a medical school. The only item added to the Decree by Judge Swope was "…preference for admission… as between applicants of comparable qualifications, shall be given to bona fide residents of Derry Township, Pennsylvania, who possess the prescribed requirements and qualifications for admission." Judge Swope believed that the restrictions of the building to be in Derry Township and admission preference to its residents were in keeping with Mr. Hershey's wishes. The lawyers and the Hershey people had been so successful in their endeavor that they were not about to argue over an item they considered to be a minor restriction..

Mr. Nurick told me that he had called the New York counsel when the presentation was scheduled and asked him if he would like to come. The New York counselor said: "You know, I advised them that this can't be done, but I would be delighted to come." He did come and as he left, he very graciously said "Gil, congratulations on a miracle."

Announcement

The announcement was made in the *Harrisburg* (PA) *Patriot* on August 23, 1963. The Hershey interests, state government officials, and officials of The Pennsylvania State University had been successful in keeping everything a secret until this public announcement. The announcement was best summarized, perhaps, by Pennsylvania Congressman John C. Kunkel in the U.S. Congress: "Mr. Speaker, an atomic bomb fell on Derry Township, Harrisburg, Hummelstown, Hershey and the 16th Congressional District last Friday, August 23…I refer to the announcement of the transfer of $50 million from the Hershey Trust Co. to the M.S. Hershey Foundation to create and maintain an area medical school in Derry Township." (*Congressional Record – House*, page 14991. August 26, 1963).

Members of the Pennsylvania State Legislature were furious. They had not been consulted, or told of the news in advance of the public announcement. Furthermore, the $50 million gift was twice the then university state appropriation of $25 million – and, TPSU was asking for more! A newspaper article highlighted their anger "Democrats Slam Plans For Medical Center At Hershey" (*Lebanon Dailey News, Lebanon, Pa, 6, Feb 1964*). Dr. Walker tried to assuage the legislators by telling them: "I will not ask you for money to build or operate the medical center." He was reminded of these words each year, in subsequent years, when he presented the appropriation request for the university to the legislature that included funds for the medical center. Years later, I asked him why he made such a statement when he obviously knew that additional funds would be required. His reply was: "*I* did not plan to ask for money because *I* planned to retire before the money crunch."

Transfer

After several years of prolonged negotiations on how much money to spend on construction and how much on endowment for operations, the foundation and the university amicably decided to transfer the funds and responsibility for the medical center to the university according to the following Court Decree:

> "AND NOW, This 17th day of December, 1968, upon consideration of the forgoing Petition of Hershey Trust Company…appearing that the administrative scheme adopted in the 1963 Decree is not essential to the achievement of the charitable purposes specified in said Decree and, on the contrary, has inadvertently and unnecessarily impeded the achievement of these purposes; and it appearing that the administrative difficulties encountered by the present Trustee and The Pennsylvania State University would be substantially reduced and, to a large extent eliminated, if the funds and assets were to be removed from the M. S. Hershey Foundation, and if The Pennsylvania State University were to serve as Trustee under and subject to the terms and conditions of this Decree…The M. S. Hershey Foundation, shall thereupon be relieved of their duties and discharged from any and all responsibilities or liabilities of whatever kind of nature…and The Pennsylvania State University…shall be and is hereby appointed successor trustee…
>
> Said funds and assets shall at all times be applied and expended for the planning, construction, operation,

equipping, administration and maintenance of a medical school to be located in Derry Township, Pennsylvania...

Said institution shall be designated as 'The Milton S. Hershey Medical Center' and preference for admission thereto, as between applicants of comparable qualifications, shall be given to *bona fide* residents of Derry Township, Pennsylvania, who possess the prescribed requirements and qualifications for admission."

Chapter 4 – Getting Started

Dr. Walker was in Washington, D. C. on April 23,1963, chairing a meeting of the National Science Board; they have very strict rules that nobody interrupts the meetings. Messages are taken and, if there's a break, you get your messages and, if it's important, you make the phone call. The secretary of the board put a little note under Dr. Walker's nose saying it's urgent for you to call this number. Well, he didn't recognize the number, and the only calls he would have made were if something had happened to his family. Nevertheless, when the break came, he returned the phone call and it was his old pal, Sam Hinkle. He trusted Sam, and always did what he told him to do. Mr. Hinkle said that Dr. Walker had to come up to Hershey (PA) right away. Dr. Walker told him "I can't come up right away. I'm running an (important) meeting that's going to last all afternoon." Well, Mr. Hinkle insisted that he come, so he finally went to the vice chairman of the board and said "This seems to be a crisis. I don't know what it's all about but could you run the afternoon meeting?"

Dr. Walker rented a plane and was flown to the small airstrip in Hershey. Someone met him at the airstrip and took him to the Hershey building. Dr. Walker walked into a meeting where the Hershey people had on their caps. Since many of the same people served on several different Hershey boards, they would have one continuous meeting, but put on caps to indicate that we are now the Hershey Chocolate Company, change caps for the Milton Hershey School, or the M. S. Hershey Foundation, etc. Mr. Hinkle interrupted the meeting when Dr. Walker arrived and welcomed him. Mr. Hinkle then got right to the point of asking him to come on short notice saying "Eric, we've decided that Penn State should have a medical school." Dr. Walker was furious. "Crying out loud, you bring me up here for that? I've told you time and again, that Pennsylvania cannot afford another medical school and Penn State doesn't need a medical school!" They started asking questions, "… could Penn State undertake such a project and, if so, how much would it cost?" Dr. Walker was becoming frustrated and said "Sam, you and I are poor boys and it's more money than we could ever envision." They persisted and asked "How much?" Dr. Walker said that "… he pulled a number out of the air and said $50 million." (I later learned that Penn State had talked about a medical school and used a figure of $25 million, so he merely doubled that amount). Mr. Hinkle looked at him with a twinkle in his eye and said "Well, I think you've got it." (Although this story differs from the well-publicized $50 million phone call, this is how it really happened).

Dr. Walker was astounded and embarrassed that he had lost his "cool" only a few minutes earlier. He quickly reflected; Dr. Milton Eisenhower had achieved his "monument" through the creation of the Commonwealth Campus System; what would be his monument? He had thought that it would be by adding a law school and a medical school to the university, but neither had materialized, and he had repeatedly, and publicly, said that Pennsylvania could not afford, and did not need, another medical school. There was now a very real chance to obtain a medical school at no cost to the State or the University. He immediately agreed to the affiliation. The Hershey people were hopeful that their *Cy Pres* would be accepted, and they needed an academic affiliation before the public announcement. The Pennsylvania State University was the only university in the Commonwealth, at that time, without a medical school, and there were none between Philadelphia and Pittsburgh, leaving a "gap" in Central Pennsylvania.

Dr. Walker then secretly contacted his Executive Committee of the Board of Trustees on May 6, 1963 and they agreed with the affiliation. Their initial thoughts were "Oh boy, we can get a medical school at no cost." However, as they discussed it, one of the committee members had some doubts, and another – who was always against all new ventures said "Look, they are trying to do you in." Dr. Walker was getting worried because he had given his word to the Hershey people that they would affiliate. However, they ultimately agreed and the Executive Committee adopted a formal resolution on July 26, 1963 and notified the Hershey Foundation that Penn State "stands ready to receive the proposal and to undertake to establish and operate…" Dr. Walker reported this to all members of the Board of Trustees on August 23, 1963 (the date of the public announcement) saying that "This information could not be released until the Court had acted on the petition." At a Special Meeting of the Board of Trustees on October 4, 1963, it was voted to adopt the following resolution:

> "RESOLVED, That there be and is hereby established, as part of the University, a College of Medicine; (the eleventh college)
>
> BE IT FURTHER RESOLVED, That the officers of the University be and hereby are authorized to negotiate such agreements and arrangements as may be necessary or desirable by the University of a Medical Center for the M. S. Hershey Foundation in Derry Township, Pennsylvania."

We had no permanent buildings except for Gro-Mor barn, Long Lane (which was being used as an administrative building), and East-Mor; however, we did have an immediate need for some laboratory space. Dr. Bryce L. Munger, the founding chair of Anatomy, established a histology laboratory in the Long Lane kitchen, recruited Ms. Aileen Sevier, as the histotechnician, and began making histology slides for the incoming class of medical students. A graduate student (William B. Rhoten) accompanied Dr. Munger from the University of Chicago to complete his Ph.D. thesis research. He had several embalmed monkey cadavers to dissect, and the formalin smell was too overwhelming for this to be done in Long Lane; so, the milk house at Gro-Mor barn became the first research laboratory on campus.

Figure 1 Gro-Mor barn (*circa* 1966), one of the first three farms purchased by Mr. Hershey for his school, and site of the first research laboratory and a mock-up of a hospital patient room.

Chapter 5 – Selection of a Site

In November, 1963, Dr. Walker met with Mr. Whiteman, Dr. Hershey, and Mr. Charles Wolgemuth (Manager of the Hershey Farms) to discuss the site for the medical center. The Hershey people had chosen a site based on availability of electrical, sewage, and water connections. There were three clusters of buildings on the land: Gro-Mor house and barn (completed 3/15/29); East-Mor house and barn (completed 4/25/36); and Long Lane house and barn (completed 6/15/36). The houses had been used as homes for the Milton Hershey School boys and were discontinued as such in 1964. All three of these units have some historical significance; Gro-Mor was one of the three first farms purchased by Milton Hershey for income to support his boy's school; East-Mor was used as a dormitory for some of the first class of medical students (they still have an annual reunion); and Long Lane was the first administrative building for the medical school. A wooden beam from the Long Lane barn was used to handcraft, by the MHS students and staff, the Mace (a symbol of authority) for the College of Medicine and is carried, with great pride, at the head of the procession at graduation ceremonies.

Upon viewing the proposed site for the medical center, Dr. Walker described it as a "very beautiful one and will make an impressive place to put a medical center." Several years later, a Nobel Laureate was giving a lecture at the medical center and commented about the beautiful site and said "This is the only time that I have given a lecture in a major institution and be able to look out the window and see cows grazing in the pasture,"). Dr. Harrell later indicated that he was involved in the site selection but correspondence in the files clearly indicate that the decision had been made before his appointment. Maybe the Hershey people just went through the motions with him to get his reaction, or to make him feel like he was personally involved.

After touring the proposed site, the Hershey people pointed out that an additional 50 acres to the West could be used for a technical center (site of the current Hershey Center for Applied Research), something that Dr. Walker had discussed with Mr. Hinkle when they

Figure 2. Proposed site for the medical center, from the East; Gro-Mor, lower center; East-Mor, center left; and Long Lane, center right.

still believed that $50 million would be more than enough to build a medical center.

Dr. Walker later, and frequently, mentioned land to be used for the medical center, using the phrase "...at a price to be determined by them." This was obviously a sore point with Dr. Walker because he thought they were undervaluing the price of the land, even though the money would go back to the Hershey Trust. It may have been a coincidence, but the Hershey Trust sought legal opinion regarding authority to lease real estate owned by the Trust. "The Facts," as transmitted by Mr. Nurick on June 8, 1964, stated: "Although the Deed of Trust of 1909 contains several provisions which make reference to the disposition of real estate held under the Trust, the express powers granted to the Trustee are set forth in Section 6 as follows"

"No part of the proceeds of the sale of any land, or of the principal of the trust as it now is or additions thereto, by gift or otherwise, shall ever be expended for any purpose whatever, except for the purchase of additional land for the purposes of the School."

Thus, a lower price would mean a lesser amount transferred back to the Trust and less to be expended from the $50 million. Perhaps the price per acre was based on the prevailing rate in the township since the money for the land would be used to buy other land that may not be as desirable, or as expensive, as the medical center site; giving credence to the real estate comment of "…location, location, location…"

Dr. Harrell did have the land appraised and it was $8,000 per acre, and he included that figure in the first construction application to the Public Health Service. At the request of Mr. Hinkle in a letter dated July 22, 1965, this appraised figure was changed to $2,500 per acre "… given the charitable nature of the Hershey Trust."

The original site for the medical center was 120 acres, with Hershey Trust retaining title to a perimeter strip of several hundred yards to the East along Bullfrog Valley Road and South of Route 322. Dr. Harrell thought this amount of land to be too restrictive, and inadequate for future growth. However, the Hershey people were quite firm in their decision. At the first Public Health Service construction site visit, Dr. Harrell showed an aerial view of the proposed medical center site in the midst of the surrounding, undeveloped land. Without any further prompting from Dr. Harrell, the site visitors started asking questions: What about future growth? Will the surrounding land still be available in the future (reminding the Hershey people that most medical schools are severely limited for lateral growth because of other buildings/ businesses on the perimeter)? The next day, the site visitors were told by the Hershey people that the site had been enlarged to 283 acres and would extend to Bullfrog Valley Road on the West and to Route 322 on the North; the land to the East and North would be held in reserve, by gentlemen's agreement, for the medical center if they wanted to buy it in the future. In later years, the medical center did buy the additional land and the site is now approximately 550 acres.

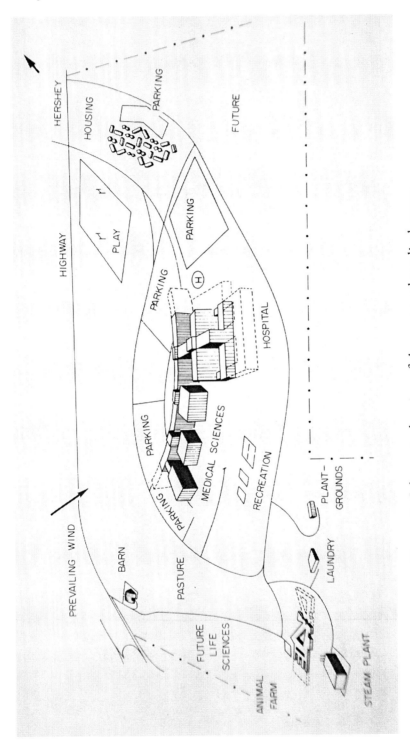

Figure 3. Schematic drawing of the proposed medical center.

Figure 4. Aerial view of the original medical center (*circa* 1973)

Chapter 6 – Advisory Committee

Dr. Walker decided to appoint an advisory committee for the proposed medical school but his problem was to find an executive director of the Committee. He was concerned that " if we find a man who is good enough to be the executive director, then he wants to be dean or vice president, and this we cannot afford to do because we still do not know what kind of school we want…when we get in touch with a man we like, we find he is tied up until next year. Therefore, we have to try to find somebody who is just between jobs because he had finished a job and not because he has been fired."

Even the name of the Committee was problematic. Should it be Planning Committee, Advisory Committee, or Survey Committee? In a hand written note, Dr. Walker stated "I want a committee that gives us advice on plans. Planning Committee suggests too much decision and control. Therefore revert to Survey Committee." It is interesting to note, however, that Dr. Carpenter, after he was appointed as the Executive director of the Advisory Committee used stationary denoting it as the "Survey Committee" whereas Dr. Walker referred to it as the "Advisory Committee" especially when using it in the context of being the group responsible for a decision that he had made. Dr. Walker had contacted several well-known people in science and medicine and all agreed to serve; they were:

> Dr. George Packer Berry, dean of the Faculty of Medicine and of the Harvard Medical School, and president of the Harvard Medical Center, Incorporated, Cambridge, Massachusetts

> Dr. James A. Campbell, professor of medicine, University of Illinois Medical Center and chairman, Department of Medicine, Presbyterian Hospital of Chicago, Chicago, Illinois

Dr. Edwin L. Crosby, executive vice president and director, American Hospital Association, Chicago, Illinois

Dr. Philip Handler, James B. Duke Professor of biochemistry and chairman, Department of Biochemistry, Duke University Medical Center, Durham, North Carolina

Mr. Samuel F. Hinkle, president and chairman of the Hershey Chocolate Corporation, and member of the Board of Managers of the Milton Hershey School and the Board of the Milton Hershey Foundation, Hershey, Pennsylvania

Dr. Richard A. Kern, president emeritus of medicine, Temple University School of Medicine and Hospital, Philadelphia, Pennsylvania

Dr. Edward D. Raffensberger, clinical assistant professor of medicine and assistant chief of Gastrointestinal Department, School of Medicine, University of Pennsylvania, Philadelphia, Pennsylvania

Dr. James A. Shannon, director of the National Institutes of Health, Bethesda, Maryland

Dr. Joseph T. Wearn, professor emeritus of medicine and former dean, School of Medicine, Western Reserve University, Cleveland, Ohio

Dr. W. Barry Wood, Jr., professor of microbiology and director, Department of Microbiology, The Johns Hopkins School of Medicine, Hygiene and Public Health, Baltimore, Maryland.

Figure 5. Advisory Committee
for a medical center of The Pennsylvania State University
(*circa* 1963)

All of the members of the Advisory (Survey) Committee were renown in science and medicine except Mr. Hinkle and Dr. Raffensberger. Mr. Hinkle, of course, represented the Hershey interests and Dr. Raffensberger formerly practiced in the Harrisburg area, was well liked, and, at least some of the Hershey people had hoped that he would return, in some capacity, to the new medical center.

Dr. C. R. Carpenter, a professor of psychology at TPSU, was appointed as the Executive Director of the Committee. He had approached Dr. Walker when he learned of the committee, and told the president "…you're going to conduct one of the greatest experiments in creative ideas that you'll ever have and we ought to find out just how this committee arrives at its conclusions…This is a great psychological experiment…I would like to take a permanent role in it…I would like to tape it… I would like to make sure that the discussions flow properly…I think this is one of the things that will go into the archives to be looked at years and years from now." Dr. Walker was persuaded although he sensed that Dr. Carpenter may have had ulterior motives. However, he was well-known in the faculty and had their respect. Also, Dr. Walker was beginning to feel some pressure from his faculty that the medical school may overshadow them; he knew that the College of Science was enthusiastic, agriculture had some medically related research projects, and engineering was working on some devices that had medical application, but the people in the arts were very threatened that some of their funding might be diverted to the new medical school.

I have been told by several individuals that President Walker asked the dean of each college to describe how they could interact with a new school of medicine, including course offerings and sharing of faculty that could be used as part of the medical curriculum. The head of the college of science library told me that he had been told by his dean to start a medical library but, after spending $87,000 had to quietly dispose of the holdings when it became clear that no part of the medical school would be on the University Park campus. Dr. Walker did suggest that the first two years could be at the University Park campus, and even assist in recruiting basic science faculty for the medical school. These suggestions were quickly vetoed; the money could only be spent in Derry Township. Dr. Walker never admitted to any subterfuge nor that he had encouraged such activities as a means to assuage his faculty.

The Advisory (Survey) Committee only met once (Dec 20-22, 1963) even though Dr. Walker had envisioned possibly five meetings. Dr. Carpenter orchestrated the whole event and it was choreographed with lights and cameras. It was the general feeling that most of the participants were uneasy and distracted by all of the lights and cameras. Mr. Hinkle was more vocal: he wrote to Dr. Walker "I believe that you and I are operating on the same wavelength exactly when it comes to matters of economy, so it seems to me we should play down future meetings insofar as the public is concerned and not have ourselves surrounded with batteries of photographers and publicity men. This is expensive and unproductive, and our funds are too badly needed to permit spending in this manner."

Mr. Hinkle was also concerned about Dr. Carpenter's role as the Executive Director of the Advisory (Survey) Committee; in a letter to Dr. Walker he wrote "I am informed that not long ago two men were sent to Hershey from Penn State to measure the dimensions of certain of our hotel rooms. Whatever their time and their travel expenses amounted to for a day is simply money thrown away because we have all of this information for the asking and consider this visit to have been a boondoggle....On Friday afternoon I gave two hours of my time to Dr. Carpenter...This is the last time I intend to do this before the selection of a Dean, and in the future I will delegate matters of this type to someone else in our group since it was all lost motion as far as I am concerned."

There are some people who thought that the Advisory (Survey) Committee had a much greater role in planning the medical center than could be found in the archives or files. Dr. Walker may have contacted them, individually, on specific issues but, as mentioned above, the one meeting that they did have was rather unproductive, primarily because of all the theatrics. However, they did have an important role in that Dr. Walker would suggest the information was coming from the Advisory (Survey) Committee when he was really using them as a cover for his own agenda thus giving creditability. This may have been his intent when he appointed them, i.e., soothing his faculty, and others, by letting them think that this "high-powered" committee was really running the show. In reality, this is not much different from any advisory or consultant group, i.e., the more important they are and the busier they are, the less time they have to really get into the "meat" of the subject and, it is usually somewhat lower in their list of priorities. I have always believed that, in any group discussions, the pivotal positions are the chair because they can direct the discussion, and the secretary to record what should have been said. In most instances, since many people do not really think and talk at the same time, they readily agree that the minutes reflect what they intended to say. Another analogy is that consultants "blow in, blow off, and blow out."

In May, 1964, Dr. Carpenter requested a leave of absence to serve as Visiting Professor in Behavioral Sciences at the University of North Carolina. Dr. Walker promptly informed the Hershey Foundation "...that a solution has been achieved with respect to the Carpenter situation...By granting this leave, this will diplomatically remove Dr. Carpenter from further participation in the medical center project." Several years later, when I raised the topic of Dr. Carpenter's role in the medical center project, Dr. Walker coyly told me "...I don't know why Dr. Carpenter left the project when it had just started."

Dr. Walker continued to seek advice from others. One such person was Dr. Russell Poor, President of the University of Florida in Gainesville, FL. I'm not sure of the questions posed by Dr. Walker, but Dr. Poor suggested, in a letter, that the Advisory Committee have at least ten, preferably twelve meetings, for a year long study of the issues, and monthly thereafter. I do not think that Dr. Walker was impressed with this recommendation; he had already decided to disband the Advisory (Survey) Committee after only one meeting because it was relatively unproductive. Also, he believed that Dr. Poor was promoting too long a period of time, and that would derail his plan for the first class of medical students to enter in the Fall of 1967.

Dr. Poor, in his letter, focused mainly on whether the proposed institution should be a "health center or a medical center," concluding that it all depended on the type of image that the university wanted to create. He believed that the former put all of the professions on an equal level, requiring a Vice President for Health Affairs for overall administration, whereas having a medical center would mean that all of the other health professions would be subservient to medicine and merely "helping hands" for the medical profession, adding: "This is the image many medical men prefer. And I daresay, several of your National Policy Advisory Committee members will so express themselves." There is no question that Dr. Pool preferred the idea of a health center, and one cannot help but wonder if maybe he saw himself as being the one in charge of it or, at the very least. a member of the already formed Advisory (Survey) Committee. There is no indication that Dr. Walker had any further contact with Dr. Poor other than thanking him for his efforts.

Chapter 7 – Growing Pains

One of the early discussions, although somewhat prolonged, between the foundation and the university was on the name of this new medical school. There was general agreement that the name of the school should honor the memory of Milton Hershey, but there were strong feelings on the part of both the foundation and the university that neither the Hershey name nor that of the university should "outshine" the other. This issue really came to a head when the Hershey people realized that they had been using lower case "t" in referring to the Milton S. Hershey Medical Center whereas the university was using a capital "T" in their name, i.e., The Pennsylvania State University. The name issue was resolved by officially naming the institution the College of Medicine, The Milton S. Hershey Medical Center of The Pennsylvania State University with the lettering to be identical. This may seem to be a minor point (i.e., does a rose by any other name still smell sweet?) but it does reflect the nervousness on the part of both entities, the trust and the university, over which was going to have the upper hand in making the final, and more important, decisions.

The Hershey people had a total commitment to The Milton S. Hershey Medical Center and, especially to the memory of Milton Hershey. This was emphasized when one of the founding chairs answered the phone in Long Lane after hours by merely saying "Hershey Medical Center." This brought a strong rebuke from the caller (Dr. Hershey) – "The name is The Milton S. Hershey Medical Center, we should never forget that."

It was initially agreed, by the foundation and the university, that the foundation would own the land and buildings and lease them to the university for one dollar a year. However, it was Dr. Walker's interpretation of this agreement that Hershey would provide the land and pay for the buildings, similar to any building supported by the state or a donor, but the university would select the architect, design the building according to program needs, and maintain the building by providing housekeeping services, cutting grass, etc. This did not sit well with the Hershey people; they were not going to let the university run the show while they were relegated to merely sit back and pay the bills. Dr. Walker finally prevailed by getting them to agree to use the architectural firm of Harbeson, Hough, Livingston and Larson (nicknamed by Dr. Walker as H2L2). This firm had developed the master plan for the University Park campus and designed several buildings on various campuses of the university. Hershey did hire the Construction Supervisor, William Christensen, who was on their payroll (specifically the Hershey Chocolate Company payroll). The university responded by hiring an architect, D. Carl Johnson, on their payroll after the Decree approving The Pennsylvania State University as successor trustee of TMSHMC on Dec 17, 1968. Fortunately, Christensen and Johnson worked superbly well as a team, with Christensen usually taking the lead role. This arrangement suited Dr. Walker because he strongly believed that any building of significance was really designed by the engineers and "all that the architects do is to put a 'tent' over it to make it look pretty." Could this belief have derived from the fact that Dr. Walker was an engineer by training?

The Hershey people mentioned that they had been approached by a planning group about a site and funds for a community college (possibly on the medical center site) with a branch in Harrisburg, PA. The Hershey people had told the planning group that they had no more money, a theme that would be repeated over and over, but would the university be interested in such a proposal? Dr. Walker responded that he thought the university would be interested but he was hesitant about having two undergraduate campuses in the same geographical area as well as a graduate program (Gov. Scranton had asked TPSU to take over the Olmstead Air Force base in Middletown, PA, and offered $1 million in state funds to build a campus because closing the base was having a very serious adverse economic impact on Central PA). Dr. Walker decided to let the matter of a community college rest since neither Hershey nor the university had the money required, and it could be an administrative nightmare trying to put them into one geographical oversight.

On Nov 21,1963, Dr. Walker met with a group of Hershey people and they raised, again, the issue of a community college. Dr. Walker's response was "No". They met again on Nov 22 to tell Dr. Walker that they were thinking about relocating the Milton Hershey School to the other side of town, freeing up the current campus for some other purpose, e.g., a community college and a technical school; they were also thinking about the public reaction when they announce the closing of the Hershey Junior College. However, they emphasized that they could not afford to give it away and would have charge something on the order of $125,000 per year for rent. Dr. Walker told them that he thought the idea had some merit but he did not think the university had the funds. Obviously, he was already having serious misgivings about the ultimate cost of the medical center.

In a memo to file (November, 1968) Dr. Walker wrote "They were now proposing that we take over the Milton S. Hershey School." but he added "Since this discussion was taking place while we were trying to adjust to the death of President Kennedy, some of my remembrance of the meeting may not be very accurate." When I questioned Dr. Walker about this he acknowledged that he remembered them discussing the possibility of TPSU running the Milton Hershey School as an educational venture, or as a hypothetical question, but he did not think it was a serious request and was only brought up as a discussion point of a much broader educational scheme.

Dr. Walker, in a memo to file dated February 10, 1964, stated: "I now begin to have grave doubts if we can operate the way I had originally planned. I doubt very much if there can be much interplay between the medical school and the university. It now looks as if the best plan might be to hire a dean and let him take the brunt of it. I think that this will mean pretty much that Penn State abdicates and allows the use of its name only." He also said"...the Hershey people still are thinking that they are going to approve all bills down to the last tea bag."

Dr. Walker met with Mr. Hinkle on Feb.20, 1964 to discuss the "problems of the medical school." Dr. Walker confided that his faculties were growing restless about the potential threat of a medical school, and what impact it might have on their funding. He had hoped that the appointment of an Advisory Committee, with Dr. Carpenter as the Executive Director (who was held in high regard on campus) would help to dispel these fears but, apparently, it was not working. He went on to say "...faculties are not people who follow easily, and even after a decision is made they do not loyally fall in behind it, but usually those who disagree continue to disagree."

Dr. Walker was also concerned about his Trustees, whom he had led to accept the medical school affiliation: "Initially, they thought of the money as an endowment, to do with what they wanted. Now, they are beginning to realize that they have taken on significant obligations and this could cost them more, perhaps much more, than the $50 million." One senses that they are beginning to feel like they are riding on a fast moving train that cannot be stopped.

Dr. Walker met with Dr. Hershey on Feb 24, 1964 at the Harrisburg Airport. "It had been decided that…would limit all conversations with the Hershey people to a channel between John Hershey and me (Walker),… Cattell and Wiegand to have no contacts, Donkin would tell Barnes… Cattell is to stop everything but the chart kind of studies that he is doing." It is very clear that Dr. Walker was becoming frustrated; there were misinterpretations, innuendos, and personal thoughts interpreted as official decisions. This did not sit well with Mr. Hinkle; he believed that a discussion with any one of the Hershey inner circle was the same as talking to all of them at one time, even though they did have individual opinions. Mr. Hinkle stated "I would not last long if I did not tell these fellows everything I know." Nevertheless, they agreed to Dr. Walker's plan of communication.

Dr. Walker went on to say "…it now appears to me that your group and mine are not only not on the same track but we are going in divergent directions." "We are used to operating frugally and efficiently, but at the same time we must operate in an academic atmosphere." He added "…we must find another method of operation…might be for the university to limit its activities to an advisory function, taking no money from the foundation and expecting none…mean that the M. S. Hershey Foundation would employ the dean and he and all subsequent staff members would be on the Foundation payroll…it would be the responsibility for the dean and the Foundation (Hershey Trust) to put together a curriculum, a staff, a student body, to get Federal funds if desired, and to attain accreditation…Penn State would be lending its name to the operation and providing a *de facto*, but tenuous, University affiliation."

I'm not sure if Dr. Walker really meant what he was saying or just using it as a bluff. Dr. Hershey asked Dr. Walker if he thought that they (Hershey) could go it alone, and the immediate response was "no."

Dr. Hershey responded "I am convinced of this also, and this is why we have to make a go of it." Dr. Walker expressed the desire to be "…relieved of any responsibility while at the same time the good will and pleasure of the announced affiliation would not be dissipated." One senses that, at least the university, was in over its head and desperately looking for a gracious exit. The Hershey people, on the other hand, acknowledged their naivete in a major program of this type and were desperately looking to the university for guidance. Despite the blunt talking, there were still problems in communications or, was it a case of the blind leading the blind?

Dr. Hershey called Dr. Walker on the evening of Feb 26, 1964 and "…talked about building faculty housing. (Dr. Walker)…warned him that…thought this was a little dangerous because faculty don't want to be housed; they want to find their own homes." Although not explicitly said, the Hershey people were concerned about local builders buying up available land and taking advantage of a housing shortage to make huge profits. ." "…(Dr. Hershey) …touched on the requirement of the use of Hershey services. First he started talking about heat, light, and electricity, and finally got into such things as milk and so forth…that he would not want us to buy Nestle's chocolate when Hershey chocolate is available. They also discussed the selection of an architect, possibility of feeding the medical students from the MHS commissary, student housing, doctor's fees, hospital and nurses. In regard to nursing students Dr. Hershey used the term of slave labor and how it could lower operating costs… I (Dr. Walker) made it very clear that this is not the way that they are training nurses today." Dr. Hershey also said that "…Mr. Hinkle was afraid we would get in conflict with someone whom I (Dr. Walker) believe produces medical doctor's secretaries who can also be medical technicians, and he did not want to compete with private industry in that manner."

Dr. Carpenter had a conference with Dr. Hershey on February 14, 1964. Dr. Hershey raised several issues: appointment of a dean, the fact that the Advisory (Survey) Committee met at University Park instead of Hershey; and a lack of communication. The Hershey people believed that the university people should spend more time on the project and meeting with them. Dr. Carpenter tried to emphasize that Dr. Walker was very busy and that running Penn State was a man-killing job.

The reply was "…but you and he have been out of town consulting." Obviously, the tension between Hershey and the university was getting near the breaking point.

The concept of the funds available for the medical center, and how they would be spent, continued to deteriorate. In Dr. Walker's memo to file he stated: " We, today, Dec 1, 1966, received a letter signed by Arthur Whiteman from the Hershey Foundation saying in fact that they intended to keep $30 million of the Foundation's money for a permanent endowment and spend only $20 million plus accrued interest on the construction; that they would tell us from time to time how much money was available for operations…This is a completely new idea and a change in the agreement, which if it had been specified originally, we would not have accepted. They are transferring responsibility for providing funds for the Center from the Foundation to the University, and we should not accept this…It should also be pointed out that the Foundation itself decided on the site of the operation, sold the land at a price determined by them, and caused the decision to construction (of) utilities at prices much higher than would have been necessary at other places…However, in no respect, was it expected that the Foundation suddenly shift the financial responsibility for the Center from them to the University. We should not accept it, and indeed, tell them if they insist. Then we should not plan to take in our first class in the fall of 1967 and immediately apply to the courts for a clarification of the agreement."

I'm not sure how much of this was actually shared with the Hershey people and how much he was just venting his thoughts to the files. However, it does reflect his peeves about the price of the land and the law-required decision to build in Derry Township instead of University Park; these issues were established facts from the beginning. Why not accept them and move on? His comments are probably a reflection of more deep-seated feelings of frustration: i.e., it is a much bigger task than anyone ever anticipated; neither the foundation nor the university had ever done anything like this before; his attempts to get meaningful advice while retaining control have almost totally failed; and the original $50 million which had seemed like a windfall and – now that costs and projected costs are becoming more real – is clearly going to be inadequate to achieve the original thoughts and goals. He must have felt like a drowning man without a life vest. One can only imagine the delays and hard feelings if he had told the Hershey people exactly how he felt and gone to the courts; not to mention the embarrassment to all.

At a meeting on July 18, 1967 Dr. Walker had prepared a statement for the Hershey Medical Committee (comprised of TPSU Board of Trustees Executive Committee and representatives of the Hershey interests but Dr. Harrell was not included). However, Dr. Walker was not able to present the statement as he had planned; each time that he attempted to do so he was side-tracked because the group kept raising questions. The primary thrust of his prepared statement (copy not available and was not distributed to those present at the meeting) was "...that we are now at a crisis point and once again we wanted to remove any implication of the $30 million residual that Whiteman had put in his letter. As a matter of fact, I am firmly convinced that we ought to soon get a commitment that more money be added to the principal – probably $25 or $30 more million." Dr. Walker went on to say "I'll admit that the possibility of this happening is fairly low, for I understand that Schiller (Vice President of the Hershey Chocolate Company and a member of the Hershey Trust) is violently opposed to it and John Hershey is too, since he is spending so much money on the development of the boys' school. I also suspect that the money is not available in the excess income fund at the present time. My guess is that some of our people feel that we ought to just stall and wait, hoping that before long something will come up that will make the money available. I am trying to point out that we won't dip below the $30 million mark until about 1969, but then we will dip very low if we are (not) really going to get the (extra) money. I want to point out that this business of start-up costs is very real and that we (TPSU) cannot be expected to supply it. Although there is some talk about going to the Legislature, I am not sure this is the time to do it...Charlie Oakes kept saying 'we must tell them that although eventually we expect to get more money from the Legislature this is not the time to do it'...I am afraid that Charlie and some of the others are just trying to postpone the evil day, where I would rather have a confrontation as soon as possible." Although the meeting appeared to be quite spirited there was no final resolution, just continued frustrations.

Chapter 8 – Recruitment

Dean

The appointment of a **dean**, or lack thereof, was a major concern to the Hershey people. Mr. Hinkle repeatedly pressured Dr. Walker to recruit a dean for the new medical school. Finally, the names of candidates began to emerge; at first one supported by the Hershey people, only to be countered by one supported by Dr. Walker.

In a letter dated Jan 2, 1964, Mr. Hinkle wrote to Dr. Carpenter that "…there was tremendous agreement upon a definite individual who would be the first choice for this spot…unless we had badly misjudged our man, which seems to me to be an impossibility at this point, I feel that we almost certainly have found the one that we are searching for." There is no reference to a name for this individual. In a subsequent letter to Dr. Carpenter dated Jan 14, 1964, Mr. Hinkle stated: "With respect to the appointment of the dean, I reiterate our opinion that this should be done without further delay. Indeed…this action is now overdue. We have indicated our choice to Dr. Walker. We were very much impressed by this individual and he meets (the) qualifications admirably. He is just the right age; he has the training, experience, prestige and status; he appears to be progressive in his philosophy and ingenuous in his thinking: he is obviously inspired by the challenge of developing this institution along the most progressive lines and in accordance with the most modern standards; and his personality and character seem to meet the bill perfectly…We at Hershey have an intuitive feeling the gentleman in question would be so attracted by the challenge that he probably would be disposed to accept the appointment. I want to stress again that if the appropriate University officials agree with our evaluation, the position should be offered immediately." Again the individual was not named.

In a letter to Dr. Walker dated Feb 11, 1964, Mr. Hinkle stated: "As to the selection of a dean, I must confess that I am somewhat taken aback by your present feeling in this regard. I came away from the meeting at Penn State, feeling that we had, through your efforts, gathered an absolutely top-notch group as a survey team. In listening for the several days to the discussions by these men, I felt that Dr.(blank – I have purposely omitted the name of some of the candidates because of some of the sensitive comments) followed very close behind Dr. Berry and Dr. Shannon in the incisive opinions that he gave during the discussions. Roy Wilkinson (TPSU lawyer) and I rode to Hershey with Dr. (blank) and, as our conversations continued, my favorable impressions of him grew, and, in probing his background, I felt that he was of the right type and the right age to head up the new school and that we were fortunate to find one of such caliber in the top flight planning group." Mr. Hinkle was responding to a letter from Dr. Walker, dated Jan 22, 1964 saying: "Now concerning the deanship. I know you favor offering the job to (blank). However, I have not proposed this to either my trustees or to you. I have within the past few weeks discussed the possibility with a number of members of the Advisory Board (sic)…a few of their comments (individuals were not named):

> 'If you are going to do it, you don't have to do it now. He will accept at any time.
>
> If you pick a dean now, you have frozen the whole plan and won't need an Advisory Committee.
>
> You can do much better than that. With this wonderful opportunity, you should not lock yourself is so early.
>
> You need a more prestidigous (sic) name and you can easily get one.'

Therefore, I just conclude that we should wait a while longer before we make the final step. As you know, I would rather go a little more slowly and be sure that we are right than to take any action which we might regret six months or a year from now."

Mr. Hinkle's response to this was: "I am surprised to read that you feel that this can be deferred and the subject approached in a leisurely fashion. My own feeling is that our progress will slow down if we do not find the right man soon, and that, when we do, we will not be fair to him if we superimpose our plans upon him instead of having him move step by step with developments. I fully agree that we must find the right man, but I do believe that this should be accomplished by the time spring comes and supervision and planning become realities."

This prompted a response from Dr. Walker to Mr. Hinkle, dated Feb 13, 1964, in which he finally explains his position: "I guess this is what cautions me about hiring deans. But I guess, too, I am conditioned by the fact that all of my fellow presidents who have medical schools warn me of medical deans. I am warned that they become irascible, power grabbers, spendthrifts, and so on. And when I hear their groans and see medical deans moving from place to place, I know that there must be some difficulties.

But seriously, when we get a dean, we are wedded to him. And when we have disbanded the Advisory Committee, his recommendations must carry much more weight than mine. If he would say we shall have 100 students per class, how can I tell him that I think 50 are plenty? If he wants a whole battery of microspectrographs, we are almost committed to buy them for him. Thus, he becomes the school, for him we buy any and all of his idiosyncrasies. This is why I feel that the broad outline should be determined first. How many students, how big a hospital, do we train nurses, do we have a full-time faculty, and so on. Until he is hired it is easy to have him participate in the decisions, but once he is hired he makes them."

Thus, Dr. Walker clearly delineates his position of preferring an Advisory Committee that he can control rather than a dean that he cannot. Mr. Hinkle, on the other hand, is very frustrated that Dr. Walker is trying to retain total control instead of recruiting a dean who knows what he is doing and lead in a meaningful way.

Mr. Hinkle responded to Dr. Walker on Feb 18, 1964 saying: "In my humble opinion, the difficulty of maintaining complete understanding between and among people is the cause of more than half of the world's troubles. Here we are, you and I, to each of whom the loss of a dime in the snow could have been of tragic importance, both being surprised at each other's approach to a common situation. Let me assure that I have not thrown caution to the wind as I think of a dean for the medical center nor do I think that you have. I agree with all that you say about the importance of finding the right man and, if he turns out to be the wrong one, we are certainly going to have to dispense with his services. This dean, whoever he turns out to be, could not force the University and the Foundation to acquiesce in proposals which are obviously grandiose or extravagant. Both of us are going to have to live with this fellow and he is going to find himself frustrated very quickly if he does not conform to our concepts of economical operation. If he should be the type who sets out to be a power grabber, he will be writing his own discharge at the same time. Our group is going to be hesitant to make any important decisions before we get to see and know this man…If you are willing to have us play dead until then, the fund will grow in size as it continues to earn, but in that case I think the whole project should slow down also." Although conciliatory, Mr. Hinkle was very firm in stating his thoughts about the recruitment of a dean.

Apparently, the fate of the dean candidate favored by the Hershey people was destined when a member of the Advisory (Survey) Committee, who knew the candidate quite well, summarized him to Dr. Walker: " I disillusioned Sam Hinkle on (blank). I know a lot about him and I talked with two of my friends (whom he named at blank). He said that when (blank) did not get his own way he would throw a tantrum. Later on he used the words 'he would pout.' He said the trouble with (blank) was that he had married a rich widow and was much mixed up in the social life in (blank), but he also never had to be tactful with people and therefore never was. He said this trait would not work in Hershey."

Another candidate had been suggested by a member of the Advisory (Survey) Committee. Dr. Walker met with the candidate at the Cosmos Club in Washington, D.C. in May or June, 1964. Apparently, Dr. Walker offered him the deanship because he wrote to Dr. Walker saying "I am extremely flattered by your offer and your expression of confidence in me…However, after considerable soul searching for the past month or so, I am still undecided about whether to accept the position of dean." The candidate was a physician, doing microbiology research and serving as an assistant dean of students in another medical school. He had built a research group and realized that a move would disrupt his research for at least five years and, perhaps, permanently. Dr. Walker proposed two scenarios; one was to stay at his current location and be a part-time dean until the new medical school had some permanent laboratory space; and the other was to relocate his research laboratory and staff to University Park (this may have been another attempt by Dr. Walker to have part of the medical school on that campus). Dr. Walker invited the candidate to University Park to meet with university officials and a few members of the Advisory (Survey) Committee, including Mr. Hinkle. However, the candidate clearly could not make up his mind. Mr. Hinkle was so frustrated, at one point he asked, "Have you ever worked as a real doctor and, if so, how do you make a decision (diagnosis)?" Apparently his answer was somewhat equivocal.

In a letter to Mr. Hinkle, dated July 13, 1964, Dr. Walker said: "I must say I had my mind set on getting (blank) and still hope that we can convince him to take the job...If he says no, then I think we must go to an older person who has already built a medical school... accept the fact that he will probably build a duplicate with small changes of what he already has. I am beginning to look at this type of candidate just in case we lose (blank)" This is a probable reference to Dr. George T. Harrell, but it is not clear whether Dr. Walker was really considering Dr. Harrell or if he was just trying to put pressure on Mr. Hinkle. Mr. Hinkle's reply on July 22, 1964 was quite pointed: "I am a little concerned...your letter where you suggest that we may have to find an older person and accept the fact that he will probably build a duplicate of his medical school of some years ago. I believe we can and must do better than this." In the same letter Mr. Hinkle begins to express more reservations (in addition to Dr. (blank) not being able to make up his mind) about (blank)'s candidacy: "I feel that he does not credit us for the results of six years of our own thinking in this connection, since I assure you that nothing has arisen which had not occurred to us and has been discussed in the past." The candidate did meet with the joint Foundation/Penn State committee on July 31, 1964 and reiterated all of his concerns and frustrations.

The Dean Search had been a contentious point from the beginning. The Hershey people thought that someone should be appointed immediately to help with the planning; Dr. Walker was more hesitant because he wanted to plan the school and its' curriculum.

On August 21, 1964, Dr. Harrell met, as an informal consultant, with a small committee of the Board (TPSU) and some of the Hershey people. Dr. Walker, in a memo to file, said that: "There was a very general conversation concerning medical education which got into the problem of ethics and legal positions of medicine...Dr. Harrell was questioned about his *bona fides* (sincerity), and told how he had gone into the medical college building business. Things were going along fine until Hinkle asked if it would be possible to get a high-class faculty in Hershey. Harrell said that it would be possible, but would not be easy. Hinkle asked 'Why?' Harrell said it would be difficult because we did not have the backup of a first class University. This made Hinkle bristle. He said, 'Why not, we've got Penn State.' Dr. Harrell proceeded to point out that having Penn State 90 miles away was not the same as having Penn State in the backyard. He illustrated the point by talking about some of the problems we had just discussed. How could a doctor (student) discuss ethics with the sociology, or philosophy or legal department when they were a hundred miles away? How could they send their students over to the biochemistry department to discuss a more complicated point under these conditions? This seemed to satisfy Hinkle and company. At the end of the meeting everybody came over and told me 'not to wait, to go ahead, this is our kind of man – we can work with him'."

The second time that Dr. Harrell met with Dr. Walker was at the Cosmos Club in Washington, D. C. and as an informal consultant, again without a fee. Dr. Harrell later recalled the experience: "Suddenly, it dawned on me…that he was getting down pretty much to concrete questions and not just broad philosophy. That's when…I said what are you trying to do, recruit me as dean? He sort of grinned and I said now look, let's be perfectly honest. This is a terribly demanding job and I'm 55 years old…If you can find somebody between 37 and 45 go and get them. I'm exhausted, and I've used up all my ideas. He said what's the matter with you, didn't you make any mistakes? I said 'Yes'. Do you know what they are? 'Yes'. You know what you should have done? 'Yes'. I (Dr. Harrell) should point out to you though that some of the things that were not done were not always mistakes. They (ideas) were forbidden by the president of the university for either academic or political reasons. I thought he was wrong and they should have been done. I would put those as frustrations…He said well, why don't you come and do it right once. I said well, I've never heard that argument before, but that's a pretty good one, I think I will." That must have been one of the shortest, and unorthodox, interviews for a medical school dean. Dr. Walker went on to add "…but with a clear understanding that if I get feedback either from my trustees, from the public or from other medical schools that these (ideas) are not right or not going well that we stop immediately." Dr. Harrell said "that's fair enough."

Dr. George T. Harrell was appointed as the founding dean of the medical school beginning Nov 1, 1964. He immediately immersed himself in the process of organizing the school, writing grants for matching construction funds, recruiting department chairs, and planning for the first class of medical students.

The only idea of Dr. Harrell's that caused some concern was when he said that one of the first buildings would be an animal research farm. Dr. Walker raised his eyebrows, but Mr. Hinkle was more specific: "after we gave him all of this money to build a medical center and then he tells me that he is going to build an animal farm – I thought that he was crazy!" Dr. Harrell explained to them that there were 14 new medical schools being developed and all would be competing for the best faculty, and a modern animal facility would be a unique enticement. Both Dr. Walker and Mr. Hinkle then understood his vision and became very supportive of the project. Another surprise to Mr. Hinkle was when Dr. Harrell told him that he planned to connect the animal research farm to the central animal quarters in the Medical Sciences Building with an underground tunnel. Mr. Hinkle thought this was an unnecessary expense. Again, Dr. Harrell explained the importance of research, accessibility of investigators to their animals, and the ability to move animals from one building to another without exposing them to variables of climate changes, plus the advantage of having utility lines (steam, chilled water, electrical, telephone and cable) accessible for maintenance, repair and expansion. Mr. Hinkle relented but requested that the proposal for the building be put out to bid two ways; bury the utility lines without a tunnel and an alternative of having the utility lines in a tunnel that could also be used for passage of people and animals. The bid for the tunnel was less than $50,000 more than just burying the utility lines. The tunnel was accepted and this investment has paid for itself many times over.

Figure 6. Construction of the tunnel, (1967)

Figure 7. Tunnel showing space being built for pipe expansion and emergency egress (1967)

The next reference to a dean is Mr. Hinkle's letter to Dr. Carpenter, dated Sept 16, 1964 (just before Dr. Carpenter departed for his sabbatical in NC), in which he states: "Here in Hershey we are all relieved and elated that have found our dean who, in the opinion of a good many people, might well be the best man in the United States for the assignment." Later, this favorable response was echoed in a letter to Mr. Hinkle from Dr. Hershey dated Feb 1, 1965: "Progress on the medical center continues to move along under Dr. Harrell's dynamic leadership. Each day one senses more and more the full measure of his stature. I tremble to think what kind of a situation (that) we would be in at this time if you had not come forth, as you did, to rally all of us to oppose a man who very nearly got the job."

When Dr. Harrell started Nov 1, 1964, Dr. Walker said "...now you don't go to Hershey right away. You come to University Park, learn about Penn State and its people. I'm going to put you up at the Nittany Lion Inn and you're going to stay there two months...I reluctantly did that...but I said...they (the architects) had to start right away and the only way that could be done was if they were next door. They (H2L2) reluctantly sent Harry Kurki up to work with me..." As Christmas approached, Dr. Harrell went to Dr. Walker and said "...I want to spend Christmas with my family and I thought that I had spent enough time on the main campus. Hershey was so much more convenient for the students and faculty that we were trying to recruit. Also, I wanted to be where I could keep an eye on the construction..." Dr. Walker agreed with Dr. Harrell's request.

The next item for Dr. Harrell was where to live. The Hershey people told Dr. Walker that they had bought a house for the dean (formerly owned by Mr. Mohler, President of the Hershey Chocolate Company, and very suitable for entertaining). Dr. Walker immediately vetoed the plan, saying; "... if the dean of the medical college gets a house then every other dean will expect to get one." The Hershey people then offered Dr. Harrell a choice (emphasizing..." the importance of handling the proposals on a confidential basis since these are special arrangements"):

> "Plan I: Small suite on the first floor at Hotel Hershey. The suite includes living room, bath, and twin beds. This would be made available to you between now and April 1 at the rate of $35 per week.

> Plan II: A corner room at the Cocoa Inn with twin beds at a weekly rate of $30.

> Plan III: A room with twin beds at the Country Club at a weekly rate of $30....breakfasts are not served at the Country Club and that noon and evening meals are not served at the Country Club on Mondays. On all of the above plans Mrs. Harrell may stay with you as little or as much as it may be convenient for her to do so at no extra cost. On any of the above three plans you you are at liberty to take a 10% discount for meals on the bill."

Dr. Harrell chose Plan I – the Hershey Hotel, and set up an office in Long Lane. He immediately began writing construction applications for matching federal funds, recruiting department chairs, and keeping an eye on the construction. During these winter months, he was often the only guest in the hotel, but it was fully staffed. On those occasions, he would be met at the door and asked if he would select his choice (from a full menu) so the kitchen staff could prepare his dinner and go home.

When Dr. Harrell arrived in Hershey, he realized that the medical center had a Hummelstown mailing address. During an earlier era, the Postmaster's salary was based on the size of their mail district. The Hummelstown Postmaster was very aggressive in his thinking and included all of the area up to the edge of Hershey in his district. Dr. Harrell decided it would not be appropriate for our address to be The Milton S. Hershey Medical Center, Hummelstown, PA so he rented a post office box (P. O. Box Y) in Hershey so we would have a Hershey address. Of course this meant that someone had to drive into town twice a day to pick up the mail for a few years until the U. S. Postal Service redistricted the area.

Dr. Harrell was a master at writing grant requests for Federal matching funds for construction and organizing the site review evaluation. The procedure is to submit an application to the Public Health Service who then select experts in the field to site visit the institution to obtain additional information, and those who are members of the parent review committee report to that committee with a recommendation, and the committee makes a recommendation of an award. Of course, Dr. Harrell knew most of the site visitors but he left no stone unturned. At the first site visit (request for the basic science wing) he checked the flight schedules of the visitors and noticed that one would be leaving home after lunch and arriving late in the evening in Hershey. None of his connecting flights served any meals and he would arrive at the Cocoa Inn after the dining room had closed. He reviewed the man's background and decided that he would like a Smithfield ham sandwich tray with an appropriate wine to be delivered to his room upon arrival (Smithfield ham was a specialty at the Cocoa Inn). Needless to say, this gesture made a big impression. At this particular site visit which was the first of several site visits for construction funds, one of the site visitors was very concerned about whether a precedent was being set. He asked: "you are requesting Federal funds for a building that will not be owned by the university, and to be built on land that is not owned by the university. What if the project fails; how will the government recoup its money." All eyes turned to Mr. Whiteman. He quietly replied that we (the Hershey Trust) would repay the money if that happened. The site visitor, somewhat astonished, said "with all of the applications that are being planned, do you realize that it might be as much as $18 or $20 million?" Mr. Whiteman replied "in that case, surely you'd give us 48 hours notice." There were no further questions on that issue.

On the site visit request for the Animal Research Farm, Dr. Harrell had organized an informal dinner at the Groff Farm in Mt. Joy, PA (specializing in serving Pennsylvania Dutch meals in their home). After the dinner we were given a tour of the house and one of the site visitors, having new bifocals, slipped on the narrow steps and fell. He insisted that he was not hurt but had some pain in his neck and back. Since there were no medical facilities readily available, Mr. Hinkle said "don't worry, we own the pharmacy." He called the pharmacist and said meet us in 30 minutes. The site visitors and some of the other medical men went to the pharmacy and obtained the medicine. The man was fine the next day.

Department Chairmen

The next challenge for Dr. Harrell was the recruitment of **department chairmen**. How do you recruit to buildings barely under construction in the middle of a field?

When Dr. Harrell was recruiting department chairs for the medical school at the University of Florida he realized that, as a medical student at Duke University, he had been impressed by the youthfulness of the faculty and, it seemed, had a high level of enthusiasm and willingness to try new ideas. He tried this at Florida and the average age of the founding chairs was 33 (at Hershey it was approximately 37). He focused on people with an M. D. degree for the basic science chairs because he thought they could relate their discipline to the clinical sciences better than people with a Ph.D.

I asked Dr. Harrell how he recruited the chairs at Hershey. He said "I would write to the chairman of three of what I thought were the best departments in their field. I said that I was recruiting and asked them for names, not only from their staff, but others that they knew. I said that I was not interested in recruiting (people who were already) department chairmen. I wanted people under that rank and I didn't say how much (under). In my own mind I felt it worthwhile to look harder at the third man in the department because the second man in the department, if he'd been there any length of time, is going to replicate what the professor has done and has been successful. Now the third man is still struggling and he may want to do things that he thinks are right but he is afraid to try it there. I was very specific that what I wanted as a first requirement is a good teacher whom the students will respond to. My candidates had to have shown potential in research and whatever they've published have been (had to be) good… In the clinical fields, then, I ranked them in the order of teaching first, patient care second and research last. In the basic sciences it was teaching, research and then whatever else they did either in activities in the school or in the community.

I would pick three possibilities from the replies, write and ask them if they were interested and if I could come and visit them. The reason that one visits them is to see what they've surrounded themselves with and the general atmosphere of their own unit. The impression you want to find here is a highly organized man who is going to do everything to the millimeter and it's got to be right… He hasn't done anything exotic; look at how the secretaries react to this man, and his technicians…when they see him coming, do they walk out of the way. You don't have to say anything, the body language says it. Obviously then they've got to be people who can get along with those they work with. If they have done it at a lower level they should continue this at the upper level."

A "must" of every interview was for Dr. Harrell to take the candidate up to the hill behind Long Lane, and overlooking the medical center site. For some of us, it was an open field covered with snow, but for most it consisted of vehicles, equipment, construction trailers, workers, and the structural skeleton of a building. Dr. Harrell would, vividly and enthusiastically, describe the building and its mission, research and patient care activities in such detail that you could begin to envision students in classes, technicians in the research laboratories, patients in the hospital, etc. This was his subtle way to see if the candidate could envision this and share his excitement of what was going to be.

Figure 8. View from "the hill" over-looking Long Lane and the proposed construction site; Gro-Mor barn is in the background (1967)

Figure 9. View of the construction site during recruitment (1967)

Dr. Harrell was very successful in recruiting the founding chairs. Almost all had tenured positions at other institutions, all were below the academic rank of professor, and had solid funding sources for their activities. None were tenured on their appointment to the College of Medicine; however, they were excited about the challenges and willing to take those risks.

Starting salaries were a bit of a problem. Many thought that the salary levels were set by the university and/or Dr. Harrell, and comparable to those in other disciplines in the university, which tend to be below those in the medical sciences. This is not entirely correct. The Affiliation Agreement between the Foundation and the University, August 27, 1964, states "All salaries of any person recruited and employed by the University, if in excess of $20,000 per year, shall have the prior approval of the Foundation." Using this guideline, Mr. Hinkle in a letter to Dr. Carpenter (February, 14, 1964) wrote "as to salary, we believe that the starting range (for the dean) should be in the range of thirty to forty thousand dollars, thirty five thousand being an appropriate figure at the beginning." It is not known how he arrived at that figure; perhaps it was in the range of the Hershey executive salaries at that time. Dr. Harrell started at $30,000 and, he later told me that he did not receive a pay raise for three years. However, Dr. Walker did provide an additional $5,000 per year in deferred pay in a special program with the Mellon Bank that was available to certain university administrative personnel. Nevertheless, it automatically set an arbitrary salary schedule of $15,000 for basic science chairs and $25,000 for clinical science chairs. This posed significant problems in recruiting since most of the candidates were already making more than that and, were at lower academic rank. The eventual salary range was $13,428 to $27,500 for basic science chairs and $29,000 to $42,000 for clinical science chairs.

The wives of the prospective chairs were also an important part of the interview process. Dr. Harrell talked to them separately and told them that "…your husband is making a difficult career choice; in addition to helping him and your children you need to realize that you are moving into a very different area. Available housing is almost non-existent; the schools are good but they may be different from what you are used to. The town has been built around the chocolate company and it is a very close, tight knit community, and very conservative; they may not know how to accept you, or you them."

Figure 10.   FIRST EXECUTIVE COMMITTEE (1972)

Seated: Vincent G. Stenger (Obstetrics & Gynecology), Richard Naeye (Pathology), C. Max Lang (Comparative Medicine), Howard E. Morgan (Physiology), George T. Harrell (Dean), John A. Waldhausen (Surgery)
Standing: Anthony Kales (Psychiatry), Elliot S. Vesell (Pharmacology), John Russell (Hospital Administration), Allen Yeakel (Anesthesiology), Thomas Leaman (Family & Community Medicine), Al Vastyan (Humanities), Graham Jeffries (Medicine), William A. Weidner (Radiology), Nicholas Nelson (Pediatrics), Eugene A. Davidson (Biological Chemistry), Bryce L. Munger (Anatomy), Fred Rapp (Microbiology), Evan G. Pattishall (Behavioral Science).

There was a certain closeness and uniformity of commitment of faculty and staff. Sylvia and I had a dinner for everyone in our two bedroom apartment and Donna and Bryce Munger had a picnic. We are the only faculty families who can say they entertained the entire College of Medicine in their home and all at one time.

The wives of the founding dean and chairs were extremely helpful in helping us to assimilate into the community which was undergoing a transformation from a paternalistic community to one that needed more, and responsible, input from its citizens. They were, in order of arrival, Jean Leaman (the only "native"), Janet Harrell, Sylvia Lang, Joyce Pattishall, Donna Munger, Shirley Vastyan, Judy Rapp, Helena Morgan, Alice Davidson, Kristen Vesell, Elizabeth Jeffries, Marian Waldhausen, Virginia (Ginny) Nelson, Anne Stenger, Pat Naeye, Donna Weidner, Joyce Kales, and Theresa Yeakel. They were absolutely essential in recruiting other faculty. They started the Faculty Wives Organization, later renamed the Association of Faculty and Friends. Several served as President of that organization (in order of election): Sylvia Lang, Joyce Pattishall, Judy Rapp, Marian Waldhausen, Helena Morgan, and Kristen Vesell.

Medical Students

Dr. Evan Pattishall, founding chair of the Department of Behavioral Sciences was asked, by Dr. Harrell, to also serve as chair of the **Medical Student** Selection Committee to recruit the first class of medical students.. Upon his arrival in Sept, 1966, he immediately started developing an application form and established an Office of Student Affairs. The first head of this office, Ms. Gaye Sheffler, had a very outgoing personality and the students just loved her. Dr. Harrell insisted that all applicants invited for an interview be interviewed by three faculty. Initially, the pool of interviewers consisted of Drs. Harrell, Lang, Munger and Pattishall. We were later joined by Mr. Vastyan and Dr. Leaman.

Although the school was being designed for a class of 64 students, we decided to limit this "pioneer" class to 40 because we still had to develop a curriculum, and recruit faculty and staff. The first class can be described as adventurers, risk-takers, and slightly older than most first year medical students. However, they were very highly qualified. If an applicant was married, Dr. Harrell insisted that the spouse also come to the interview. Dr. Harrell met separately with the spouse and made it very clear that they understood the rigors of being a medical student, as well as in their future career.

Figure 11. The first Medical Student Selection Committee; (left to right) George T Harrell Dean; Evan G. Pattishall, Behavioral Sciences; Al Vastyan, Humanities; Bryce L Munger, Anatomy; Thomas Leaman, Family and Community Medicine; and C. Max Lang, Comparative Medicine (1967)

Curriculum

Although very few faculty were on hand, we had to develop a **curriculum**. At that time the university was on a term system, four terms in a year with most students taking three terms, late August through early June . Early on, we decided to teach the core curriculum in the first two terms, leaving the third term for electives. This was an educational innovation that we thought would enable each student to tailor their own education according to interests. However a noble idea it was, most departments did not have enough faculty to offer a wide variety of electives and gear up their research programs at the same time.

The tuition, at that time, was $525 per term, or $1575 per year (the same as at the University Park campus) and a real bargain in comparison with the tuition charged by other medical schools; in essence, a type of scholarship for all students.

There was considerable competition among the department chairs for the number of class hours available. One chair insisted on having the same number of hours as the more traditional departments such as Anatomy, Biochemistry, Microbiology, Pharmacology and Physiology. I later asked him why he was so insistent, and how he would fill all of the hours if he got them. His response was that if his department had less hours, the students would consider it less important than the others. I told him that I thought the quality of time far outweighed the quantity. After hours of wrangling over the number of hours for each subject, Dr. Harrell finally said "I am going to ask you one more time how many hours are required for your subject because what you have said so far simply is not going to work." The first person asked was Dr. Morgan, chairman of physiology. He replied "I can teach it in about 45 minutes; I don't know how much they will learn, but I can teach it in 45 minutes." That dissolved the debate.

A few weeks before the start of the first class, we were informed that all courses had to be approved by a University Senate Committee. All of the basic science chairs traveled to University Park with Dean Harrell to meet with the committee, who were taking their job very seriously. As it turned out, they were more interested in how the courses were numbered, i.e. 100 – 400 series were undergraduate and 500 series were graduate level courses, than they were in course content. Their reasoning was that a student could register for courses in the medical school and, after taking a few courses be admitted through the "back door." We were equally concerned about that but felt that our graduate students needed to take some courses given to the medical students. This was resolved by agreeing that all courses required for the Doctor of Medicine degree would be 700 level courses and, if the same course was required for a graduate degree it would also have a 500 number but neither would count for the other degree even if it were the same course. As a result of those discussions, we developed a general rule for several years that graduate students in the College of Medicine would not be permitted to apply to our medical school (although the lecture portion of the course was one and the same, the laboratory portions often had a different focus).

The pioneer class of medical students started classes September 25, 1967.

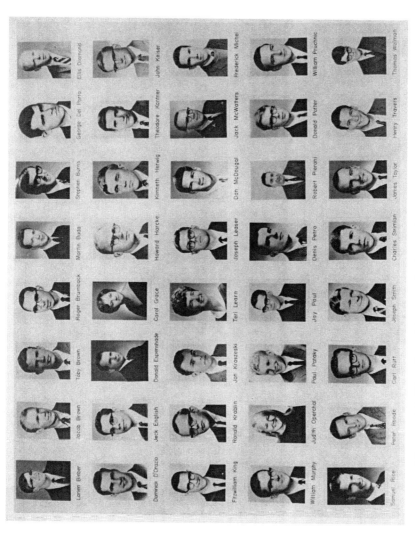

Figure 12. The first, "Pioneer," class of medical students, 1967

Chapter 9 – Developing a Program

The design of any building begins with a descriptive program, i.e., a blueprint of what you hope to achieve and, since most buildings are in use 50 + years, they must be designed to adapt to changing needs and requirements. The basic tenets in the design of a building, in addition to a program of use, are: (1) efficiency of use and maintenance; (2) flexibility of use, and (3) future expansion in a way that will not adversely affect – but complement – efficiency and flexibility. Too often, one tries to compress everything into the design. It is far better to omit complete units and add them later when the need is more apparent and funds become available.

Many buildings are designed using a standardized format and, when it is finished, decide what you want to do with it. The process should be just the opposite, i.e., decide what you want to achieve in the space being built, then develop a design accordingly. This program should be written, and published, so that future users can have a starting point of what was intended, and the possibility for change when it is required.

The design of The Milton S. Hershey Medical Center is clearly described in a book (*Planning Medical Center Facilities for Education, Research, and Public Service. George T. Harrell, 1974. The Pennsylvania State University, University Park, PA)*. A few points developed in this book should be emphasized:

> "The needs and the availability of funding led to emphasis on construction of facilities for research with primary attention to laboratories and equipment for that purpose rather than for teaching. Little initial thought was given to supporting facilities, such as animal care units, which are necessary for dependable biologic research, or for specific requirements of teaching hospitals."

> The point made by Dr. Harrell is that most medical centers start with the wrong concept by omitting, or at least not giving, equal emphasis to education, research support units, and teaching hospitals.

"The primary responsibility of a university is education. A university promotes scholarship and generates new knowledge as an integral part of the educational process...facilities...must be specifically designed for each aspect of the program, but the overlap between them requires that...the entire project (be seen) as a coherent whole."

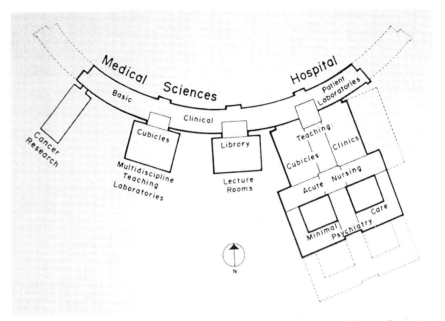

Figure 13 Relationship of functional units at Hershey, showing possibilities for initial expansion.

"The design should emphasize to students and faculty that whatever is learned and discovered in the physical plant has social relevance only if it is applied in the community where the health professional lives and and works...patterns of practice should be those which may be used ten to twenty years in the future.

"Although the university has the responsibility for education, the student has an individual responsibility. The emphasis in the educational program should be individual learning. The facility should permit the student at any level to develop his own pattern of study which he can follow the rest of his professional life.

"Learning is a subjective phenomenon and retention of knowledge is related to the intensity and duration of the exposure to information as well as repetition of the learning experience.

"Students...should recognize from the beginning that they have committed themselves to a life-long process of self-education."

Figure 14 Student cubicles at Hershey,
showing arrangement in a "street"

"This philosophy led to the concept of study cubicles, i.e., a 'mini' office where the student develops a pattern of self education using lecture notes (patient history), textbooks, a few journals/reprints, computer, and perhaps, a microscope. It is a place to review collected information, consult a few references and make a decision (diagnosis). Hopefully, this will establish a life-long pattern of self education.

"Group study was encouraged in the new medical center by the use of informal interchange areas; space that belongs neither to the faculty nor the students, a neutral place for...interchange of ideas...day-dreaming, or discussions between students...and faculty (e. g., following a lecture)... and other staff.

"The basic criterion in design is flexibility for conversion of laboratory and office space from initial to other use with change in program and function after the building has been completed and used.

"The location of future additions, both lateral and vertical, should be considered in the original design to provide for expansion of the same function found in the initial construction (for new programs)."

The key to flexibility in a building is its mechanical system (air handling, electrical, plumbing, etc.). This was achieved at Hershey by designing a series of 54 square feet, nine story (two below grade and seven above) buildings with pie shaped areas (called chases) constructed in between for the vertical distribution of utilities; resulting in a crescent design of the overall building. Interestingly, the crescent design avoided the appearance of a long hallway. The access doors and panels to the utility chases were painted in alternating colors so they could be used for directional purposes. The basic design of the medical sciences building was on a 4 feet, six inches module (in the Animal Research Farm, it was 4 feet). This means that every dimension of space is equally divisible by that module number, facilitating decisions on room sizes and laboratories, and to avoid the placement of supporting columns within rooms.

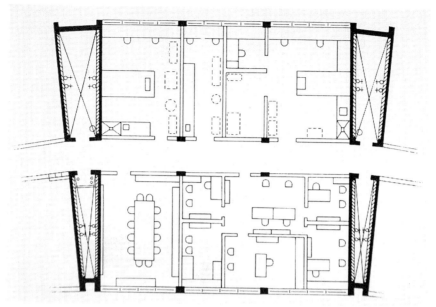

Figure 15 Plan of a 54 square feet unit at Hershey, showing pie shaped areas for utilities, and sample elements of a department or division.

Attention to detail cannot be minimized. Few people are able to conceptualize space, i. e., look at blueprint drawings and visualize ultimate function in a three dimensional manner. This is why we have architects. However, architects may be more than happy to let individuals "design" their own space because then it is not their fault if it doesn't work as anticipated, i. e., they only did what they were told.

Dr. Harrell, founding dean of the new medical center, both at Florida and Hershey, was a "master" at conceptualizing between drawings and function; so much so, that many people think of him as a builder of medical schools, rather than as an educator, which is how he wanted to be remembered. Dr. Harrell was the 1973 recipient of the Abraham Flexner Award for Distinguished Service to Medical Education. He was specifically cited for "...a true genius in his ability to develop a medical education philosophy and then translate it and interpret it architecturally...the design of the Animal Resource Facility at Hershey has been characterized as visionary and is being copied as a model throughout the world."

There are many subtle aspects in the design of The Milton S. Hershey Medical Center. For example, location of the Department of Behavioral Sciences on the first floor of the medical center emphasizes its role as a basic science; a precursor of many illnesses. Another innovation is the location of the Department of Humanities on the first floor, suggesting to students the origin of medicine in religion, philosophies of different religions and cultures. Again, placement of the Department of Family and Community Medicine between the basic sciences, especially the Department of Humanities, and the clinical specialties to emphasize transition between the patient and their family to the ultimate need for advanced treatment and technology.

Another element of the design was to enhance the view from the windows towards the community, reminding students and faculty of their ultimate responsibilities to the public. This concept was also incorporated in the patient rooms in the hospital so the patients could look out at rolling farmland and woods.

The academic departments are located by floor and discipline to facilitate transfer of new knowledge from basic science research to clinical trials to patient care, and the reverse in the case of illnesses not responding to conventional treatments. For example, the Department of Physiology is on the fourth floor of the basic science wing adjacent to major research programs in cardiac physiology; the fourth floor continues in the clinical sciences wing with cardiology and cardiothoracic surgery specialties and cardiology diagnostic laboratories; and patients with cardiovascular illnesses are on the fourth floor of the teaching hospital. This arrangement emphasizes "…the continuity of basic science with clinical research as applied to patient care."

Location of the library in the center of the building reflects previous knowledge as the center of learning; another concept important to Dr. Harrell. He felt strongly that "…the student must become familiar with the accumulated knowledge of the past which has been collected in the library…there is something about having the book in your hand and stumbling on other interesting articles."

There are other subtle innovations in the teaching hospital such as location of the nurse's station between three hospital wings on each floor, like a hub with spokes in a wheel, to emulate a smaller hospital atmosphere and enhance or facilitate visibility down each hallway. Another is placement of the sink in the patient's hospital room. In most hospitals, it is located against a wall requiring the nurse or physician to turn their back to the patient to wash their hands upon entering or leaving the room. At Hershey, it is located at an angle so the nurse or physician can face the patient while washing hands; the two occasions that patient observation is most important, i. e., the anxiety expressed on the patient's face when one is entering the room, and the lingering unanswered questions on their face when one is leaving.

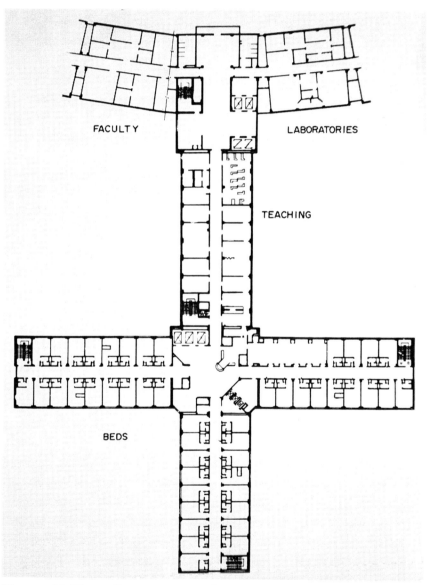

Figure 16 Plan of acute-patient floor at Hershey, showing relation to hospital laboratory wing and medical sciences building. Note the location of the Nurse's station in the center of three hospital wings

Dr. Harrell also believed in mockups/samples of various rooms and furniture before they were built/purchased. A former living room in Long Lane (initial administrative building for the medical center) was used for prototypes of the student cubicles and chairs. Each of the then faculty was asked to try them out and render an opinion. Dr. Harrell surveyed our medical students and found that approximately 14 % were left-handed, so that percentage of student cubicles were made for left-handed students.

The first hospital patient room was built in the hay-loft of Gro-Mor barn. This prototype was used to try all proposed equipment. One early mistake caught in time was that several proposed hospital beds would not fit through the doors to the hospital room; thankfully, this error was altered before 350 such rooms were built!

Dr. Harrell's knowledge of program description and building design was gained from his experiences as a student in a new medical school (Duke University) designed without a definitive program; the first clinical faculty appointment in a new medical school (Bowman Gray of Wake Forest University) that utilized an existing community hospital; the founding dean of a new medical school (University of Florida); and founding dean of Hershey where he could correct the mistakes made at FL.

At the time it was built, The Milton S. Hershey Medical Center had more space devoted to teaching than any other medical school in the United States; perhaps in the world. An important element of this space designation was eligibility for matching funds for construction, i. e., it was federal funds of 75 % for teaching space and 50 % for research space, the remaining percentages to be supplied by the awardee institution..

Ground was broken for the medical center construction on February 26, 1966 – 18 months after the announcement of $50 million for this project. It would be interesting to know the true thoughts of those participating in this ceremony. I asked several of them and they said that they were excited about something coming to fruition. I suspect that they must also have had a few lingering doubts about the future; however, they could only hope for the best.

Figure 17 Crowd gathering for the groundbreaking (1966)

Figure 18 Groundbreaking – February 26, 1966. (left to right) Eric Walker, President of The Pennsylvania State University; Samuel F. Hinkle, Hershey Trust Company; Captain R. W. Roland, President of The Pennsylvania State University Board of Trustees; Arthur R. Whiteman, Hershey Trust Company; George T. Harrell, Dean of the College of Medicine, The Pennsylvania State University

Dr. Harrell insisted that the construction site be landscaped as the buildings progressed A sensitive man, he was aware of the impact of building (bricks and mortar) on the psychological well-being and temperament of those working in these structures.

Chapter 10 – Construction

The Milton S. Hershey Medical Center was built on beautiful, rolling farmland in Central PA. The Construction Supervisor, Mr. William Christensen, said that the site was a "sea" of tripods when he arrived in 1965. This part of Pennsylvania has a lot of limestone caverns at various depths under the soil surface and they had made test borings to determine their locations. They then had to dig holes until they reached solid rock. These holes, for the concrete caissons to support the building columns, were 3-5 feet in diameter and ranged from 3 to 80 feet deep. A good portion of each hole was fractured rock with holes in it, rather than "solid rock" as defined in the contract documents; but its removal was as costly as "solid" rock. These holes were dug by hand using a tripod at ground level with a pail on a rope pulley and a man at the bottom. This was not a job for someone who weighed more than 120 pounds or who had claustrophobia! They now have machines that can drill holes of this type, but that was how it had to be done at that time. Mr. Christensen described it as "1890's technology moving at an 1890's pace." The "hole diggers" were paid an additional premium of 50 cents an hour and the men were considered to have the "badge of honor" for doing this work. The contractors brought in men from Philadelphia to dig the holes because they couldn't get local people to do it. Thankfully, the work was completed without injury or harm to the hole diggers.

Mr. Christensen described the subsurface soil conditions on the proposed site for the medical center as "…normal subsurface conditions in limestone, but this area is the worst I've ever seen…Surface water, or fluctuating ground water, causes an opening in the soluble bedrock and begins to pull the earth overburden down into the opening. The earth begins to arch above the bedrock, and the underside of the arch keeps falling off until it breaks through the ground surface as a sinkhole, which can be from a foot or less to many feet in diameter and depth, so that foundations for a structure are endangered."

To deal with the problems of the limestone subsurface, they formed a foundation design team comprised of a structural engineer, Mr. Nick Gianopolus; geologists Dr. R. M. ("Pete") Foose and Mr. Jim

Humphreville; and soils engineer, Mr. Felix Kitlinski. They had core drilling made at 100 foot intervals across the entire building site. As a result, and study, of these core samples Mr. Christensen said "...the entire facility was moved to the west to avoid a deep hole in the bedrock which indicated sinkhole activity; and a decision was made to found the structure on caissons (circular concrete piers) from three feet to several feet in diameter...excavated to solid rock, and a definition of 'solid rock' was developed. Rock would be 'solid' and acceptable for a caisson if three test probes drilled at the caisson bottom encountered no opening over twelve inches in ten vertical feet... The need for this concern with foundation design and construction was brought home rather forcefully during the construction when a post indicator on a fire line north of the building broke during the night and about one million gallons of water from the reservoir south of the medical center flowed through the break and caused a huge sinkhole in which the tops of the caissons were exposed." Mr. Christensen said that he then "withdrew my objections to portions of the elaborate core drilling program after seeing the sinkhole and realizing, with relief, that the structure was founded on 'solid' rock."

At the beginning of construction, the site was relatively level with the existing building called "Long Lane" (a former MHS home and the first administrative building for the new medical school.); this building is now "up-hill" from the medical center buildings.

The entire site had to be "re-sculptured" before the building could commence. The summer of 1966 was one of the hottest and driest on record, and the plume of dust from the earthmovers could be seen as far away as Harrisburg, PA (15 miles). The administrative building, Long Lane, had no air conditioning and the windows had to be kept closed because of the dust. Even then, one had to dust off the desk, typewriters, etc about every hour. Although the outdoor temperature was often over 100 degrees F, it was a relief to just go outside. The dust got inside the telephone in my office, causing it to cut-off, but only if I was on a long-distance call. The telephone repairman (one of two who worked for the Hershey Telephone Company and were members of the candy makers union) took it apart, looked at it, and started to put it back together. I asked him if he found the problem. He said "No, I'll

Figure 19. View across the construction site towards Long Lane, the initial administrative building for the medical center, July, 1966

just give you a new one." I asked him what he would do with the old one, thinking that they had a repair shop and would find what was wrong. He said "Oh, I'll just put it in a house that doesn't make or get long-distance calls; we know who they are and it won't be a problem." A simple solution that could only happen in a place like Hershey!

The Hershey Foundation insisted that the overall project be divided into five phases (the order of completion was Phase II, IV, I, III, and V):

Phase I   Basic Science
Phase II   Steam Plant
Phase III   Clinical Sciences
Phase IV   Animal Research Farm
Phase V   Teaching Hospital

This arbitrary division into phases, plus the requirement that contractors had to be within 25 miles of the construction site meant local contractors who could then be able to obtain financing for the job and local workers, making for excellent working relationships. Ultimately, there were 42 prime contractors, with 28 on site at one time during peak construction. It was an excellent community-oriented project. Even today, I run into people who proudly say "I helped to build the medical center." The contractors and their laborers expected to continue to live and work in the community after the medical center was built, and local unions cooperated with local contractors much more readily than they would have with a big "outside" contractor. This minimized labor disputes and, as Mr. Christensen said, "A miracle on a project of this size."

Figure 20. Construction of the Basic Sciences Wing (phase I), 1966

The owners of the general contractors were on site almost every day, especially the Ritter brothers, Mr. Wallace Alexander, and Mr. G. R. (Barney) Sponaugle. Mr. Christensen described them as "living their job." Seeing their "big bosses" on the building site also impressed the laborers on the importance of the task at hand.

One Saturday morning, I noticed steam coming out of the steam plant that was under construction. This appeared, to me, to be an unusual occurrence. I tried to call Mr. Christensen and others but to no avail. Finally, I called Mr. Sponaugle, the owner of the mechanical

Figure 21. Construction of the Medical Sciences Wing (Phase III) and completed Basic Sciences Wing (Phase I), 1967

construction firm; he said "Stay there, I'll be right over" (he lived in Hershey). He drove up in his Cadillac a few minutes later, opened his trunk and took out a tool box. He looked at me and said "It's alright, I have my union card in my wallet." He rushed into the building, climbed a ladder, and began making adjustments. After he had finished, he came out and thanked me profusely "...because it could have been a major problem if you had not noticed that something was wrong." Mr. Sponaugle's response was typical of all of the contractors and laborers on the construction team, i.e. they had a deep, personal interest in the project.

During the construction of the medical center there were a lot of decisions that had to be made on the spot, e.g., there was an electric line, plumbing line and an air duct all shown in the same place on different drawings, or there was a small pipe where a bigger one was required or vice versa. Even though immediate decisions were required, there were relatively few mistakes. Mr. Christensen agreed "...that there were an 'uncommon' number of such decisions because of the phased construction (with construction proceeding in one area while design was underway in others); the speed required in design and construction; and because of the arrival of new members of Dr. Harrell's staff with, understandably, their own concepts (requirements) of their areas." The contractors "loved" the resultant change orders, but they did add to the overall cost of the building. The contractor already had the job through competitive bidding and, when they got a change order, they figured every possible cost, added ten percent in case they forgot something, and added ten percent profit. Mr. Christensen gave credit for controlling these costs to Mr. Bob Cranage and Mr. Andy Pataky, the representatives of Stewart A. Jellet (mechanical/electrical consultants) and H2L2 (architectural firm) respectively, as full-time, on-site people.

On February 23, 1967, the building caught fire (fifth floor of the Basic Sciences Wing – Phase I). Mr. Christensen and Mr. Charles Ward, managing partner of H2L2 were in Indiana on an expediting trip concerned with limestone for the building exterior. "We returned to our hotel and learned that my staff had been trying to contact me for several hours…upon learning the news of the fire, I turned to Charlie Ward and we both, simultaneously, said 'Oh boy, there goes the schedule!'…the next day I saw laborers and iron workers cleaning up the most awful mess that I had seen since World War II – pieces of charred lumber and twisted, blackened reinforcing bars were piled on the fifth floor, and the blackened propane gas bottles were scattered over the surrounding farmland. Those who had been on site during the fire told me that gas explosions tumbled those tanks through the air like huge mortar shells…one of my staff said 'it was a real fire!'…they were using a standard system (of) propane heaters with open flames and canvas tarpaulins, used to protect the concrete, so that it would cure properly in the cold weather. As I understood it, a laborer was replacing a gas tank when a blowing tarp(aulin) touched the flame. I'm glad I wasn't there." There wasn't a whole lot that anybody could do, unless they were on the burning floor. The faculty (Harrell, Lang, Munger, and Pattishall) were interviewing prospective medical students and saw the fire, fire trucks desperately trying to hook up to the fire hydrants, and laborers up on the floor throwing gas tanks off the side of the building. Dr. Harrell, who was also interviewing a prospective student-and was very focused-looked out the window, saw the fire and nonchalantly assured the student "Oh yes, we will open on time."

Mr. Christensen added: "Those people (laborers) should get medals. John Hutton (his assistant) told me a couple of those men literally risked their lives pulling burning tarpaulins off...miraculously, the damage was not too great, and no one was injured. The stair landing slabs on the west end had to be removed and replaced, but the balance of the fifth floor was acceptable structurally. However, all of the fifth floor had to be refinished because the combination of water and fire had spalled (ruined the finish of) the concrete."

Figure 22. The "Great Fire" on the fifth floor of the Basic Sciences Wing (Phase I), February 23, 1967.

Later, Mr. Christensen said "We were able to provide at least a semblance of a medical school on schedule in September, 1967 because of the efforts of people, including the heroes in the Hershey Fire Company and Ritter Brother's labor force...Other factors which contributed to successful completion were the spirit of cooperation and expertise of the building team; the forbearance and cooperation of Dr. Harrell and his staff and the attitude of the people in the pioneer class who began medical school surrounded by confusing, noisy construction...they were risk takers, entrepreneurs looking for the excitement of a new school."

Figure 23. (left) Aftermath of the "Great Fire". Exploding propane gas tanks "hurdled through the air like giant mortar shells"

However, completion for occupancy had been uncertain. Mr. Christensen told me that he and Charlie Ward, managing partner of H2L2 (architectural firm) were standing on an embankment of the teaching wing about two weeks before classes were to start and "... ruefully saying never had we seen a major project as unfinished so close to occupancy and use;… the foundation walls were not even backfilled." The state Department of Labor and Industry had to inspect the building and, if in compliance with safety standards, issue a certificate of occupancy. They agreed to put off their inspection until Friday before classes began on Monday. One of the inspectors, who was rather large, became stuck between some scaffolding and the wall in a stairwell. All of us were thinking, "Oh boy, we are in trouble!" The scaffolding had to be dismantled before the man could be freed. However, we were approved subject to a punch list of minor items that had to be completed. The contractors and their foremen were in the building that weekend correcting all of the items. We did open on time, and as scheduled.

Immediately after the opening for the first class, things began to slow down. Finally, Mr Hinkle, on October 26, 1967, wrote a letter to the major contractors (Herre Bros, Ritter Bros, and E. C. Ernst) saying "…we find ourselves in a situation similar to the letdown of a football team, where the coach and/or special circumstances at the time have the players 'sky-high' before the game and after winning over great obstacles, they find it hard to get up enough steam for the game scheduled the following Saturday." The contractors got the message and the fast pace of construction resumed.

The Teaching Hospital, however, did not open on time. Several months before the contract completion date, Dr. Hershey and Mr. Christensen told Dr. Harrell that the hospital would not be ready for the pioneer class at the start of its third (clinical) year-owing principally to change orders. Dr. Harrell had anticipated this delay in completion and made contingency plans with Polyclinic and Harrisburg Hospitals for the third year clinical rotations. Mr. Christensen said "The decision to tell the dean was a tough one, the last thing that a contractor wants to admit is that he can't meet a schedule."

The cost of building the medical center was a matter of great concern almost from the beginning. The Hershey people had thought that it would cost about $20 million for building, leaving $30 million as an endowment for operating costs. Dr. Walker consistently estimated at least $30 million for building, and later said that would be the minimum and at least $8 million for start-up costs. Dr. Walker based his estimates on a 1964 report on medical education facilities that was prepared by the U. S. Department of Health, Education and Welfare. Dr. Harrell had served as chair of that committee.

Dr. Walker had expressed the opinion that funds probably could not be secured from the Federal government because there were several other medical schools in Pennsylvania. In later years, Dr. Walker often referred to the $20 million that "he received" from the Federal government. However, Dr. Harrell wrote the applications for construction funds; there is no evidence that Dr. Walker reviewed the applications although the Hershey people did; and Dr. Walker did not participate in the site visit reviews but he was willing to be available (the Hershey people did participate).

On January 20, 1972, Mr. Roy Wilkinson, Esq., attorney for The Pennsylvania State University (TPSU), wrote a letter to Mr. G. Albert Shoemaker, successor to Mr. Captain (Cappy) Rowland as Chairman of TPSU Board of Trustees, with regard to the financial plight of The Milton S. Hershey Medical Center.

> "The original sum of 50 million dollars was thought to be enough to build (25 million) and endow (25 million) the entire operation. At the very beginning, both publicly and privately, Dr. Walker made it quite clear that the University did not contemplate putting any of its money or the Commonwealth's money into the construction or operation.

> There is no doubt that the Hershey group thought the $50 million dollar figure was enough to build and endow the medical school. It could be that the reason it was low may have been that it was based on the cost of the construction and operation of a large hospital complex of the Mayo Clinic type, not a medical college which is more expensive to build and very much more expensive to operate...over the years the matter of the cost of a medical school at University Park had been considered in a general way from time to time... general figure of 25 million dollars had been used... by the time the suggestion came from Hershey the

figure had not been updated to reflect the increase(s) in construction costs, as well as inflation. Further, there was considerable duplication of facilities required when the construction took place at Hershey rather than University Park. ...Finally, there has been and continues to be a great increase in costs due to new developments in medicine.

Several times in the early days critical decisions had to be made by the Trustees of Penn State as to whether to proceed with the project or to abandon it as impractical. The University insisted the hospital would cost 22 million dollars. The Hershey group insisted it wold (sic) not cost more than 17 million. It was finally decided that we would 'build what we needed and pay what it cost.' ...became apparent that, in addition to everything else, start-up costs, including a full census in the hospital, were going to take a substantial bite out of the continuing endowment...it was decided that we must proceed and 'let the chips fall where they may.' During this entire period many felt that the Hershey group would 'come up' with more money as capital or 'pick up' the deficit...there never was any basis for this assumption. All the official statements were made and re-emphasized that 50 million 'was all there is, there ain't no more.' When the magnitude of the operating deficit became apparent it was clear that this incorrect assumption could be corrected only by having Hershey disassociate itself from the Trust...The...Board voted to authorize the officers to secure court approval for the University to accept complete responsibility..."

Mr. Wilkinson sent a copy of this letter to Dr. Harrell on the financial history of The Milton S. Hershey Medical Center. In his cover letter, he said: "This is for your private information. No doubt in due course you will see it or hear of it officially. I understand Mr. Hinkle has seen it and may prepare to supplement it." There was no comment on this letter or a response in Mr. Hinkle's files.

Those of us on the faculty were aware of some of the financial problems but certainly not to the extent of their magnitude. It is not entirely clear just how much Dr. Harrell knew about the problems but, if any, he chose not to share them. This was probably wise because if these problems had become widely known, they would have had a disastrous impact on recruitment and retention of faculty and staff.

The project expenditures (as of June 30, 1973) of the medical center are shown in **Table 1.** The original project consisted of Phases I – V. Phase VI (Cancer Research Wing) was one of the first planned expansions.

Table 1
The Milton S. Hershey Medical Center
The Pennsylvania State University
Project Expenditures
June 30, 1973

	Basic Science (Phase I)	Steam Plant (Phase II)	Clinical Science (Phase III)	Animal Research Farm (Phase IV)	Teaching Hospital (Phase V)	Cancer Research (Phase VI)	Total
Land	$ 98,937	$ 6,129	$ 104,191	$ 17,511	$ 211,008	$	$ 437,776
Land improvements	298,497	26,270	154,428	48,104	1,099,806		1,627,105
Construction contracts	9,552,860	3,156,002	9,109,434	1,553,937	24,333,218	3,328,608	51,034,059
Site survey & soil investigation	10,297	5,178	10,354	20,004	11,536		57,369
Architect's fees	404,555	129,313	412,862	64,054	1,064,413	216,359	2,291,556
Consultant's fees	52,188	10,507	21,394	4,751	139,417		228,257
Supervision and inspection	72,463	13,768	86,908	12,088	272,600	17,000	474,827
Movable equipment	1,138,901		1,461,392	140,643	3,762,943		6,503,879
Other	78,329	17,209	76,628	13,456	142,145	30,978	358,745
TOTAL	$11,707,027	$ 3,364,376	$11,437,591	$ 1,874,548	$31,037,086	$ 3,592,945*	$63,013,573
Federal grants	$10,211,800			$ 614,000	$10,500,000	$ 2,000,000	
Gross square feet	200,170	12,000	211,640	38,356	443,245	61,700	
Project cost per gross square foot	$58.49	$28.04	$54.04	$48.87	$70.02	$58.23*	
First occupied	Oct. 1967	Oct. 1967	Oct. 1968	Sept. 1967	Oct. 1970	Sept. 1974†	
Date accepted	Sept. 1968	Nov. 1967	Sept. 1969	Mar. 1968	July 1971		

* Estimated cost
† Estimated date available for occupancy.

Chapter 11 – Community

In 1960, the census for Township of Derry – the location of Hershey - was 12,388; in 2000, it was 21,273. In keeping with the tradition of a small town, Hershey was and is, an idealistic, model community. Mr. Hershey planned it that way for his employees. He encouraged home ownership, through loans from his bank, because he believed that home owners took more pride in their homes than renters did. However, it definitely was not a "factory" town; nor was it parochial, probably because the hockey rink and park attracted, and still do, a lot of people from Central Pennsylvania. The theatre runs features that you couldn't get outside of New York City. However, before the medical center, it had started to change. Hershey had been a paternalistic town; Hershey had always provided everything, including utilities, a bank, grocery store, lumber yard, drug store, department store, recreation, schools, a trolley, etc. Mr. Hershey wanted every convenience for his employees; they did not have to patronize them, or even live in the town, but they were there for them at competitive prices if they wanted them. The Hershey Estates credit card could be used to buy groceries, gasoline, lumber, ice cream and dairy products, laundry, electricity and other utilities. I even used it to pay the hospital bill when our oldest daughter was born.

Mr. Hershey built these facilities for his employees as the need arose and were still in place when The Milton S. Hershey Medical Center was built and planned:

Hershey Bank	Chartered 1905	1986 – merged with PNC Bank
Hershey Drug Store	Opens 1905 (Cocoa House) New building – 1963	1987 – closes
Hershey Laundry	Opens 1908	1935 – new building 2006- Building Dismantled
Hershey Department Store	Opens 1910	1973- Closes, building remains

Cocoa Inn	Opens 1910 as Hershey Inn and remained Community Inn -1936 Remolded and renamed Cocoa Inn-1958	1970- Closes, building dismantled
Hershey Telephone Company	Opens 1910 Incorporated 1935 as Hershey Telephone Company	1969- Sold to Continental Telephone Company
Hershey Electric Company	Opens 1912	1980- Merges with PP&L
Hershey Water Company	Opens 1913	1976- Sold to American Waterworks Company
Hershey Consolidated School	Opens 1914	1980- closes, building remains
Hershey Cemetery	Opens 1917	Remains
Hershey Garage and Gasoline		1988-Closes, building dismantled
Hershey Lumber Company		1971- Closes, building dismantled.
Hershey Tea House	Opens 1922	Building dismantled
Hershey Creamery	Opens 1930	1986- Building dismantled
Hershey Community Building	Opens 1932 (dedicated 1933)	1982- closes, building remains
Hershey Sports Arena	Opens 1936	Building Remains
Hershey Stadium	Opens 1939	Building remains

Mr. Hershey built 34 enterprises, collectively known as the Hershey Improvement Company. The name was later changed to Hershey Estates, and is currently named Hershey Entertainment and Resort Company (HERCO). As Mr. Hinkle said of Mr. Hershey "...lack of education made him so seemingly modest yet vain enough to name everything Hershey that he could see in the area." These enterprises were not very profitable; some years some of them made money, and in other years, they had deficits. However, it was not Mr. Hershey's intent that they should make a profit, but to serve his employees as long as they could reasonably break even. Mr. Hershey literally ran these enterprises and his company out of his pocket, or I should say his checkbook; his 1912 passbook showed a balance of $898,000 (about $17 million in today's money).

Mr. Hershey offered to build a community kitchen as well as a single church, the finest that could be built if the churches could get together. Of course, these things were impossible. In 1915, Mr. Hershey presented each of the five churches in Hershey with a gift of $20,000 to help them pay off their debts; he also predicted that it would not be long until they would again be in debt! The five churches were: Derry Presbyterian. Spring Creek Brethren, First Evangelical United Brethren (today, First United Methodist) Holy Trinity Lutheran, and St Joan of Arc Catholic. He also left an endowment of $750,000 to the public school system.

It was a beautiful town, but many inhabitants always felt that they should have more. When asked about this, one of the Hershey people explained to me that, at least some of, the town's people felt that Hershey should provide everything, including leadership. Even before the medical center, the Hershey people were making a very conscientious effort to get the township to provide their own leadership rather than to be dependent on them. Mr. Harold Mohler, successor to Mr. Hinkle as President of the Hershey Chocolate Company, told me "...there is nothing more difficult than explaining something to someone who isn't interested in understanding...it's much easier for the average person to be critical than to be logical."

It was a very stable town where people were born, lived, and died. When my wife and I came to Hershey in 1966, there were no houses for sale or rent; and there were less than twenty apartments in town.

Fortunately for us, one apartment was empty. This lack of housing was a major problem for new faculty and staff.

The realization of a medical center, with its accompanying population, caused considerable angst in the minds of the town's people. The Hershey inner circle was a close, tight knit social group, extremely conservative, and who were used to a town run their way. The local townspeople were not so concerned about their employment, but how would these new faces and ideas transform their town? One day Dr. Harrell mentioned to me, in passing, that the local community was concerned about the "outsiders" moving into "their" community. That evening, I relayed this information to my wife. By coincidence, she had

Figure 24. Hex sign on Gro-Mor barn

visited the Hershey Library that day and was very impressed with their collection of material on Pennsylvania Dutch customs, including hex signs which are prominently displayed on barns in Central Pennsylvania. This was very new to us, she having been raised in NC and me in IL. We got the idea of making a hex sign with the basic design of keeping away disease, and counter imposing on it the head of a dog, a monkey, and a rat suggesting that animal research helps to keep away human disease. This large sign was painted by a hex sign artist in Lancaster, PA and the fire department used their aerial ladder to put it up on Gro-Mor Barn, where it remains to this day. The local Hershey weekly ran a story about it. As a result of this gesture, the local people decided that we "outsiders" weren't all that bad and were trying to "fit in."

The local medical community had concerns of their own; the Hershey Hospital was going to be closed when the medical center opened (*The Philadelphia Inquirer, May 16, 1965*). The Hershey Hospital was losing their accreditation. Although it provided excellent patient care, it simply was not up to the current technology standards. Dr. Harrell had met with the accrediting people and said: "Look, why don't you postpone your decision until the medical center opens and people have an option. Then, Hershey can close it and you won't have to take any drastic action." It was agreed that this would be the plan. The local medical community became more upset when they learned that Dr. Harrell was planning on a full-time staff and they would not have admitting privileges unless they were members of that full-time staff. Dr. Harrell believed strongly in having full-time faculty who could devote their primary energies to education. The medical group met with Dr. Harrell and Dr. Walker, who completely supported Dr. Harrell, and expressed their concerns. Dr. Harrell responded by explaining that this would be a teaching hospital, and all patients would be for teaching purposes. They countered with a proposal that 50 of the 350 beds be used as a community hospital for their private patients to replace the 40 beds that they were losing when the Hershey Hospital closed. Dr. Harrell said "No." (If he had agreed to their request, it would have meant that one-seventh of the hospital would not have been eligible for matching federal funds.) Dr. Harrell offered a compromise: he was willing to accept them if they joined the planned Department of Family and Community Medicine as full time faculty, and if they had good patient records that could be used for teaching purposes. He was willing to accept the fact that they were good physicians on the basis of patient satisfaction. However, he realized that none of them had any teaching experience; they would have to spend at least six months, at their own expense, doing a mini-residency at a major teaching hospital and he would help them in arranging this experience. The local physicians were not happy with this decision but ultimately realized this is the way that it would be. Only one of the local physicians, Dr. Thomas Leaman, agreed to be a full time faculty member, and later became chair of the new department, at first in an acting capacity. Dr. Leaman expanded his private practice by adding two physicians with the same criteria required of him, i.e., being full-time and taking additional training for teaching experience; they were overwhelmed with new patients. This caused some concern among the Hershey interests when their employees could not be seen by this group because they had a full patient load. Dr. Harrell explained that it was not their intent to provide patient care for the entire community. They countered this argument by saying "you have physicians in the basic sciences, i.e. Morgan, Pattishall, Munger, Vesell, and Naeye; send them down here to see patients. Again Dr. Harrell said: "No, this is not what we recruited them for; they are here to teach and build their own departments."

Epilogue

It has been almost four decades since the gift of $50 million from the Hershey Trust to establish The Milton S Hershey Medical Center, and two decades since interviewing the primary individuals involved in the process. In this passage of time one cannot help but be impressed by what almost did not happen.

The excess accumulation of funds would not have occurred had it not been for the business acumen of Milton Hershey. Yet, here was a man who, after many business failures, sold his caramel factory for one million dollars and, unlike most of his peers of that era, not only invested it all in a new venture, but even had to borrow more money.

The business was very successful and, because of World War II, his beneficiary – the Milton Hershey School-- could not recruit enough orphans nor obtain sufficient rationed supplies for their maintenance without gradually decreasing their enrollment.

None of the men (Whiteman, Hinkle, Nurick, Hershey) involved in this momentous decision aspired to anything other than merely doing their best at their current employment and implementing Mr. Hershey's wishes. Mr. Whiteman thought he would be a house painter but developed into a financial wizard under Mr. Hershey's tutorage. Mr. Hinkle, the son of a pharmacist, had no other experience with medicine or educational ventures. Mr. Nurick, at a young age could not see his future beyond working in a factory, then – because of changing circumstances – life as a school teacher, and ultimately a lawyer. After reviewing the concept of changing Mr Hershey's will was deemed impossible (by some of the best legal minds in the country), Mr Nurick made the change possible, which was considered by many to be a landmark in legal history. Even the courage of the Judge of the Orphan's Court, Lee F Swope, to make a decision of concurrence against all odds, is remarkable because he saw the law as a right of the people and not merely as rules and regulations. Dr John Hershey rose from a house-parent/farmer to coordinate one of the largest projects undertaken in Central Pennsylvania. Bill Christensen, construction manager, ended up with the job because of a spur of the moment decision to make a detour on a trip from California to New Jersey to visit a friend. It is widely acknowledged that his expertise resulted in a quality product built at an unbelievable pace.

Dr Walker, as President of The Pennsylvania State University, was a charismatic and challenging leader but was clearly out of his element when it came to developing a medical school. He had never been associated with a medical school and its special needs in his academic career. Dr Harrell, the founding dean had not planned on a college education, much less medical school. Yet he became one of the leaders in medical education with a unique ability to translate function into bricks and mortar. His decision to recruit a veterinarian as the first faculty member and the Animal Research Farm as the first functional building completed (second after partial completion of the Steam Plant) became a major factor in the success of the artificial heart program.

How were these people different? The most recognizable outward trait was their humility. Their goals were always for others and not for themselves. Other traits were their honesty and extremely high ethical standards and a penchant for hard work. The assimilation of these people at the right time, the right place, and under the right circumstances had to be more than serendipity. The closest analogy is Divine Intervention. The Impossible Dream may be an understatement.

Yes, there were significant problems before the building opened for the first class in September, 1967. Some would say that these problems were tumultuous, ranging from thoughts of delaying the project to a complete cessation. However, due to the strengths of the individuals involved, the differences were eventually resolved in an amicable manner.

The Impossible Dream did become a successful reality over the next few decades, but not without significant difficulties. But, those too, were eventually resolved because the founders laid the proper groundwork, and chose the right people to make it work.

C. Max Lang
March 28, 2009

Breinigsville, PA USA
18 January 2010
230936BV00001B/2/P